Electing the President, 2000

Electing the President, 2000

The Insiders' View

Edited by
Kathleen Hall Jamieson and
Paul Waldman

PENN

University of Pennsylvania Press

Philadelphia

10 9 8 7 6 5 4 3 2 1

Published by
University of Pennsylvania Press
Philadelphia, Pennsylvania 19104-4011

Library of Congress Cataloging-in-Publication Data

Electing the President, 2000 : the insiders' view / edited by Kathleen Hall
Jamieson and Paul Waldman.
    p. cm.
  ISBN 0-8122-1802-7 (pbk. : alk. paper)
    1. Presidents—United States—Election—2000. 2. Political campaigns—
United States—Case studies. I. Jamieson, Kathleen Hall. II. Waldman,
Paul.
JK526   2001
324.973/0929—pcc21
                                                        2001041461

Contents

Introduction

Making Sense of the 2000 Election

The contest to elect the forty-third president of the United States was the costliest in the nation's history. With the outcome uncertain for thirty-six days after the nation voted, it was also the longest general election in the country's history. In those thirty-six days, public attention to politics rose above the levels of the campaign itself as voters and those who had stayed home expanded their vocabularies to include chads (hanging, dimpled, and pregnant), ballots (butterfly and other), votes (under and over), and voting machines (punch card and optical scans).

"The election of 2000 will be scrutinized and debated for generations," wrote the political staff of the *Washington Post*. "Did the right candidate win? Was the election stolen? Many Democrats believe it was. Republicans angrily reject that claim, but many of them were hurling charges of larceny themselves when it seemed possible that the Democrats would prevail in Florida's recount."

The 2000 presidential election was among the closest in American history. In a year in which just under 50 percent of those eligible voted, the popular vote went to the Democratic ticket of Vice President Al Gore and Connecticut Senator Joe Lieberman by a margin of just of over 500,000 or 50.3 percent of the two-party popular vote, and the electoral college to Texas Governor George W. Bush and former member of Congress Dick Cheney after a thirty-six-day standoff when Florida's 25 electoral votes were awarded to the Texas Governor.

The election was officially ended by a single vote in a 5-4 Supreme Court decision that effectively gave Florida's disputed 25 electoral votes to Governor Bush. Following a Florida statute that it said "requires that any controversy or contest that is designed to lead to a conclusive selection of electors be completed by December 12," the Court held that "Because it is evident that any recount seeking to meet the December 12 date will be unconstitutional for the reasons we have discussed, we reverse the judgment of the Supreme Court of Florida ordering a recount to proceed."

The election night outcome came as a surprise to some. On the eve of the election, most polls showed a close race with Bush ahead. There were two exceptions. The CBS News/*New York Times* poll and the Zogby/MSNBC poll gave Gore the edge. Behind the scenes Republican strategists signaled that the Bush camp expected to win with as many as 320 electoral votes. Two hundred and seventy were required to take the presidency.

For scholars, 2000 was an election that put the standard political science models to the test. For many years political scientists have endeavored to create models that would predict the outcome of presidential elections using only information available before the campaign begins in earnest. In the past, these models have usually been accurate. At the American Political Science Association's convention in late August and early September 2000, a panel of distinguished scholars of American politics factored such elements as the economy, public opinion, and the popularity of the incumbent president into their models and emerged with the unanimous forecast not that the popular vote would be close but that Gore would achieve a significant win.

On the night before Election Day, November 6, 2000, political analyst Mark Shields noted on *Newshour with Jim Lehrer* that by looking as if he was going to lose the next day Gore was "breaking every political scientist's heart." After the election, the brightest and best of the forecasters mused about the failing of their models in the March 2001 issue of *PS: Political Science and Politics*. As political scientists Larry Bartels and John Zaller put it, "some observers, including some of the most prominent election forecasters, have concluded that the problem was not with the forecasting models but with Al Gore as a candidate." Some concluded that Gore should have worked harder to take credit for the good economy. Others said voters were ignoring the economy. Still others said that voters were turned off by Gore's populist claim that he would fight for "the people, not the powerful."

In a ten-hour seminar held at the Annenberg School for Communication of the University of Pennsylvania on February 10, 2001, scholars and students of communication, rhetoric, political science, sociology, and education gathered with strategists from the Bush and Gore campaigns to try to make sense of the strangest election most had experienced in a lifetime of electing leaders and studying politics. On some points the Gore and Bush strategists agreed. At the close of the primaries Gore failed to consolidate his advantage while Bush made good use of his time to reposition himself for the general election. The Gore campaign's "get out the vote" effort was superior to that mounted by the Republicans. On other areas they disagreed. Each side argued that it had the advantage on the issue of Social Security.

There was talk as well about why the predictions of the political science models had failed. Among the explanations was the possibility that the models failed to distinguish between incumbent president Bill Clinton's job approval rating and his personal popularity. Using the second in the models instead of the first produced a more accurate forecast, argued some of the consultants.

We also learned what decisions the consultants regretted. President Bush's top adviser, Karl Rove, reported that his candidate should not have taken a Sunday off the campaign trail in the final ten days. Gore adviser Carter Eskew regretted that Gore's call for permanent resident status for refugee Elian Gonzalez stepped on the campaign's message. Voters were unwilling to credit Gore with the nation's prosperity, argued the Gore strategists. The Democrats should have aggressively seized credit for the economy, argued the Republicans. The Democrats' frustration that the Republicans had coopted the Democratic issues of prescription drug benefits and education was palpable. The Republicans considered September their most difficult month—a time, in the words of one, of "rats, moles and bad polls."

The debriefing also confirmed that the election was fought over the same territory. "We spent our money pretty much in the same states as the Republicans," said Gore adviser Bill Knapp. And each side had its own grievance with the media coverage of election eve, with the Republicans arguing that their candidate had been hurt by the mistaken early evening network call of Florida for Gore and the Democrats contending that the late night call of Florida and the election for Bush effectively framed the thirty-six days of discussion about the outcome as the sore loser, Gore, trying to usurp an office he had in fact lost. In good-humored exchanges the two sides maintained that each had in fact won. "We certainly believe we won the election," said Gore's Carter Eskew. "I learned today that we lost," laughed Republican adviser Alex Castellanos.

Among the purposes of the election debriefing was the eliciting of information that would prove helpful in interpreting the results of the Annenberg 2000 Survey. In an effort that began in November 1999 and extended through Inauguration Day 2001, we conducted over 100,000 interviews, asking Americans about their political knowledge, media use, and opinions about candidates and issues. Designed by Richard Johnston and Kathleen Jamieson, and supervised by Princeton Survey Research Associates (PSRA), the survey used a rolling cross-sectional design predicated on continuously interviewing throughout the campaign season.

The sorts of issues that interested us included disentangling the effects of media coverage from the effects of campaign events. For example, our survey shows that those who did not watch the first presidential debate were more responsive to news analysis about the debate after the fact, and over time the commentary led some to see Bush's performance as more positive and Gore's as more negative. Pundits and news accounts had more influence on voters who didn't watch than on those who did. While commentators attributed George Bush's seeming rise in the polls following the first debate to dissatisfaction with Al Gore's performance, Americans who watched the debate continued to believe Gore had performed better than Bush; but among those who didn't watch, there was a significant drop in perception that Gore had won.

In the days after the first presidential debate, among those who did not watch it, 43 percent gave Gore the victory while only 21 percent gave Bush the victory. Among those who did watch, people also gave Gore higher marks than Bush, with 43 percent saying Gore performed the best and 36 percent saying Bush performed best. One week after the debate, among those who didn't watch, those giving Gore a victory dropped 6 percent to 37 percent, while those scoring Bush as the winner jumped 5 percent to 26 percent. One week after the debate, among debate viewers, the perception who won hadn't significantly changed.

The focus on lapses by Gore affected the perception of those who did not watch the debate; while those who did watch trusted their experience and held to their conclusion that Gore had won. Why? Gore adviser Bob Shrum argued that "the Bush team did a really good job, fair and square, of capitalizing and jumping on the so-called misstatements the Vice President made in the debate. . . . The Bush campaign's skillful exploitation of some of the mistakes did drive the press coverage of the debate, which then influenced many millions of others who had not seen the debate."

The varying interpretations of the debates highlighted the struggles each campaign faced its quest for the White House. Insiders from both campaigns would agree (perhaps with some reservations) that the conventional wisdom about the nature of the 2000 race was largely correct: Al Gore had an advantage on the issues, while George W. Bush was seen as the more likeable of the two contenders. Gore pollster Stanley Greenberg made a strong case that in a wide range of policy areas, a majority of American voters not only were closer to Al Gore's position, but perceived that the Democrat would do a better job advancing their concerns.

Nonetheless, the Bush campaign did not concede ground on issues, even ones in which Democrats have traditionally held a clear advantage. As Bill Knapp, who created advertising for the Gore campaign, said, "It was a constant frustration to us that you would make progress on education. Bush spoke about education from the heart, it seemed sincere, it seemed real. That was a problem for us . . . we really couldn't find an effective way to blunt his education offensive."

The most notable issues on which Bush trod into traditional Democratic territory were Social Security, long known as the "third rail" of American politics (touch it and you'll be zapped), and Medicare. Although the differences in the two candidates' plans may have been complex, the Bush campaign moved aggressively on these issues, airing a number of contrast ads both advocating their position and attacking Gore's. Knapp described one Bush ad criticizing Gore's prescription drug plan as "a real pain in the neck. It took us a couple of tries to get the response to that down right." Bob Shrum also noted "the refusal of the Bush campaign to just cede the issue. They engaged on the issue, we reengaged. In the data, we won the issue. But we had to spend time on it." Bush advertising consultant Mark McKinnon described the underlying theme behind Bush's engagement on issues such as education and Social Security: "George W. Bush is a different kind of Republican. This is not the kind of Republican that you're used to. He's reaching across old boundaries and borders, talking about issues you're not used to hearing Republicans talk about."

But issues were only part of the story in 2000. The campaign was in large part a competition of definition: each side labored mightily to define itself and to define the opponent. Among the fundamental questions each side framed were, Was Gore honest enough? Was Bush up to the job?

The Gore strategists believe that their most successful commercials portrayed the candidate as a "fighter," taking on powerful interests in defense of ordinary people. Carter Eskew argued that this portrayal accurately reflected the Vice-President's true feelings. "One of the things that people perhaps did not understand about the Vice President, and that they found jarring, and at times even hypocritical, is the fact that he is by roots a populist. He is what I used to call a technopopulist. In other words, he can sit down and talk to you for four hours about the human genome, but the end of it will be, '. . . and we've got to make sure these insurance companies don't screw people with this information.'" When it came to the Texas governor, the Gore campaign struggled to find a compelling attack on Bush's level of preparation for the job of president that did not sound mean-spirited. "Trust me," said Bill Knapp. "We tested ad hominem attacks against him. They were not effective. We tested spots about the draft. We tested spot after spot where we showed his screw-ups and his inability to communicate smoothly and effectively. We used that technique in '96 against Dole very effectively, but we could not get ads that worked well in 2000 against Bush for that."

Like the Democrats, the Republicans argued that their most effective messages accurately reflected their candidate's personality and character. In describing Bush, advertising consultant Alex Castellanos said, "We've seen the first New Republican. There was a time the Republican Party was this dark force, very dark and pessimistic and anticommunist and anti-this and anti-that. . . . This time, there was a fellow who, by his very nature and personality, said, 'Hey, not only are we going to talk about moral values, and right and wrong, and not only are we talking about tax cuts, but I care. I like people. I want to help.'" Unlike the Democrats, the Republicans found a certain type of personal criticism—that focusing on Gore's honesty—to be so effective that they made it an increasingly central message as Election Day approached.

Independent polling confirmed the importance of personal characteristics in voters' decisions in 2000. According to Kathleen Frankovic, who directs the CBS News/*New York Times* poll, "People who claimed that issues mattered more were more likely to say they were voting for Gore. The people who said personal qualities mattered more were more likely to say they were voting for Bush. In fact, there were more 'personal quality' voters who said they were voting for Bush than 'issues' voters who said they were voting for Gore. But if you asked the question a different way, you saw issues diminish in concern and importance. We asked: 'What matters more, a candidate agreeing with you on important policies, a candidate's honesty, or a candidate's leadership?' Given that choice, only 7 percent chose policy agreement and four out of ten opted for honesty."

Looking back, the advisers saw a number of places where different decisions could have been made. Karl Rove argued that the revelation of Bush's DUI arrest led to the campaign's loss in Maine—but said not revealing the incident earlier was "a decision that I agreed with and a decision I'll defend." Bill Knapp lamented the fact that the Gore campaign was outspent in Florida by $10 million. "Now I don't know that much about paid media," said Knapp, "but I know that 10 million dollars is worth 537 votes."

Electing the President, 2000: The Insiders' View digests a unique day-long discussion in which top strategists from the Bush and Gore campaigns explained their decisions, questioned each other, took questions from scholars and students, and wondered about what might have been. To it we add a first look at the election seen through the filter of the Annenberg 2000 Survey and a time line chronicling significant general election events. If how we elect is as important as whom we elect, understanding the most disputed election in a century and a quarter is a particularly worthy endeavor. We thank the scholars, students, and consultants who made this volume possible. Their remarks were edited to clarify the sorts of ambiguities that characterize extemporaneous presentations and exchanges.

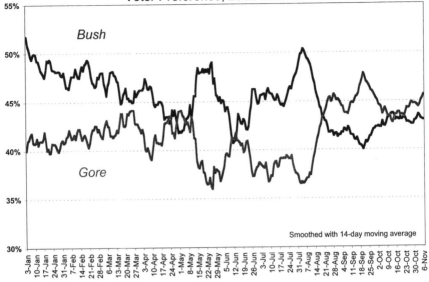

Voter intentions, Campaign 2000

Election Timeline

March 14	Bush and Gore clinch nominations in six Southern primaries
March 30	Gore advocates permanent resident status for Elian Gonzalez
April 20	McCain says SC flag should be removed, admits political pressure made him afraid to say so before.
May 1	Gore and McCain meet to discuss campaign finance
May 5	Gore and Bush take stands on gun suits
May 9	McCain endorses Bush
May 12	Bush introduces free trigger lock program in Texas
May 15	Bush details plan to allow investment of Social Security benefits
May 16	Gore criticizes Bush's Social Security plan
May 20	NRA convention: Charlton Heston criticizes Gore
May 27	Gore gives commencement speech at West Point
June 1	Bush grants stay of execution to Ricky McGinn for DNA tests

June 16	William Daley takes over Gore campaign
June 21	Gary Graham executed in Texas despite controversy
June 23	DOJ official recommends independent counsel for Gore fundraising
July 5	Gore attacks drug companies
July 11	Bush addresses NAACP
July 12	Gore addresses NAACP
July 13	Bradley campaigns with Gore
July 20	Gore visits Texas to criticize Bush
July 24	Bush picks Cheney
July 31	Republican convention begins
August 3	Bush accepts nomination
August 7	Gore picks Lieberman
August 14	Democratic convention begins
August 17	Gore accepts nomination
August 25	First Bush attack ad—prescription drugs
September 1	Republican ad attacks Gore's credibility (TV on counter)
September 4	Bush inadvertently insults *New Tork Times* Adam Clymer
September 8	Bush agrees to negotiate debates
September 11	Gore appears on *Oprah*
September 12	"Rats" ad revealed
	Bush injects "subliminable" into lexicon
September 16	Agreement set on debates
September 19	Gore dog prescription drug story breaks in *Boston Globe*
	Bush appears on *Oprah*
September 21	Gore calls for release of Strategic Petroleum Reserve
September 23	Bush gives strongest attack yet on Gore credibility
October 3	First debate
October 5	VP debate
October 11	Second Bush/Gore debate
October 17	Final debate
October 24	Rand releases study criticizing Texas education
November 2	Bush DUI story breaks
November 7	Election Day

One

Matthew Dowd
and Fred Steeper

*Matthew Dowd served as President Bush's director of polling and
media planning during the 2000 campaign. Prior to joining the
Bush team he served in that same capacity as a partner in Mav-
erick Media. He also was one of the founding partners of Public
Strategies Incorporated, an international public affairs firm. Mr.
Dowd is currently a senior adviser for the Republican National
Committee.*

*Fred Steeper is a partner at Market Strategies, where he di-
rects the electoral politics side of the politics and public policy
group. A nationally recognized expert in political behavior and
electoral research, Mr. Steeper has conducted research and con-
sulted for numerous Republican state governors and U.S. Senators and Representatives since 1972. Mr. Steeper was the senior
polling consultant for the George H. W. Bush 1988 and 1992
presidential campaigns and has also been involved in a wide
range of public policy research.*

MATTHEW DOWD. There is something called an urban legend. If you drink Coke with Pop Rocks, your stomach will blow up. There is also something I call an urban political legend. If something is repeated enough, has been in the newspaper, or is said by somebody of stature, it becomes true, and everybody repeats it.

Once that happens, consultants and campaign operatives make decisions based on some urban political legend. I'm going to refer to some of these that I think people assume to be factual but which, if you go back and look at what actually happened, they aren't true. They became "true" because everybody repeated them, including people at seminars. I hope that we'll set the record straight. That's part of what I want to do, so people can make judgments about this campaign based on what actually happened.

I will focus on several key moments. These were points in time where crucial decisions had to be made, that could have gone one way or the other and in some way affected this race. Obviously, this race was one of the closest in history. The net popular vote was a bigger margin than in some races, but percentage-wise it was one of the closest races in history. Some of these decisions did have an impact on the race.

At various times Vice President Gore, by actions or words, reinforced negative perceptions. I'm going to point out three or four instances where things he did or said confirmed in people's minds, at least temporarily, what they disliked about him. There were three or four important instances in which the Vice President reinforced a negative perception. In politics, one of the things you learn when a candidate does that is that it is significant. When a candidate reinforces a perception, either positive or negative (not through a TV ad the other side runs or anything we do), it has a tremendous impact on voters.

We planned a general election strategy from day one. The primary was really a part of that general election strategy. Anybody who watches hockey knows how this works. A hockey team plans the regular season as if it's going to be in the playoffs. This campaign was planned from the start as if we were going to be in a general election. The primary was part of that plan. We didn't want to do anything in the primary that could affect the playoffs, but we ran into the "straight talk express." We had to reconfigure, which I'll talk about in a second. But from day one, we knew which states were going to be important.

When we put together memos in the summer of '99, we knew that West Virginia was going to be a key state. A lot of people were surprised about that. We knew Tennessee was going to be a key state, and in spite of what the press said, we thought Florida was one of the key battleground states. We had a list of twenty or twenty-two states. Florida was always on that list.

We never assumed we would carry Florida for sure and wouldn't have to worry about it. We always considered Florida crucial to the election and a part of our general election strategy. By contrast, New Jersey was never on our list of targeted states. Having looked at past patterns, we took New Jersey off, and it wasn't one of the twenty or twenty-two states to focus on.

There were four or five key primary events. Raising money was an important key primary event that we won. The amount of money we raised put all our Republican primary opponents on the defensive. At the same time, endorsements built momentum that Bush would be the likely Republican nominee. Press coverage was a big part of building that momentum. The public polls done in July 1999 were important for our efforts to build momentum.

Although there was not a lot we could directly influence about the public polls, all the press coverage we generated put other Republican candidates on the defensive in raising money and other things they needed to do. In these areas, we won in the early stage. Our other assumption was that Forbes was going to be the candidate we'd be running against. One big reason we passed up

Matthew Dowd. Photo by Kyle Cassidy.

federal matching funds was the fact that we thought Steve Forbes had an unlimited capacity to spend money and to run TV ads, as he had against Dole in 1996. That was a big reason why we opted not to accept matching funds and thus be bound by spending limits. The other was that we didn't want to end the primaries with no money left over like Dole in 1996.

If we passed up the public financing, after March we would be able to raise money to run the campaign before we actually got the nomination. But then McCain came along like a skyrocket and changed everything. Forbes didn't spend nearly as much money as anybody thought he was going to. He never really caught on. We did have to fend off a lot of things that Forbes did; he was attacking us, arguing, among other things, that our tax cut was not big enough. Meanwhile, McCain was attacking us for the tax cut being too big. So while we still had to worry about Forbes, McCain became the candidate to deal with, primarily because of the press.

Round one: Iowa. Basically, we finished in Iowa where we thought we'd finish. We never thought we'd blow everybody away in Iowa, but we thought we'd get the percentage that we got. Iowa was done on the ground. New Hampshire was not. McCain caught on, he was very popular, and his people ran a great campaign in New Hampshire. The independent turnout for him on Election Day was unreal, and this affected some of the other states down the road.

We were very worried about McCain, obviously, but as more states came on after New Hampshire and Michigan, the Republican base and Republican registration minimized the independent impact. But New Hampshire was horrible. When the first exit polls came in, we were down by 20. Mark McKinnon said, "Well, can it get any better?" We all looked at each other and said "Well, we might get to 18 down."

We ended up losing by 19. It was dismal. We all knew what was going to happen in the press the next day. We were going to be portrayed as stupid, and all the decisions that we made were dumb, and we spent more money than any candidate ever in history, and we lost New Hampshire. We didn't want to read the newspapers. I remember flying back from New Hampshire to Austin the day after. I wanted something to read, but the loss was on the front page of every newspaper, every section. I couldn't even read the sports section because sportswriters will use lines like "The Philadelphia Seventy-Sixers trounced the Clippers like Bush was trounced in New Hampshire." So I picked up the *New York Times* obituary section and read that. (Actually, if anybody reads the *New York Times* obituary section, it is very well written.)

Delaware was important for us because it took us from being knocked out to having an eight count. Although the state was small, it affected the campaign internally by demonstrating that we could win a primary after having been knocked down in New Hampshire. It demonstrated to the press that this thing wasn't over.

Round two: South Carolina. Delaware helped us come out of New Hampshire, but when we got to South Carolina (we thought New Hampshire was bad!) the published polls had us five down in South Carolina. South Carolina was supposed to be one of the first fire walls, the second being Michigan. It was horrible. It affected the campaign internally. But South Carolina helped turn the campaign around. Governor Bush went back to what he does best, delving into the crowds, something he kept doing right through the general election.

One thing I want to correct: our campaign and McCain's spent about the same amount of money on television in South Carolina. A lot of people think we overwhelmed them with media and television, but we spent roughly the same amount of money in South Carolina. There was a lot of third-party activity going on, but mediawise, we spent about the same amount of money.

Round three: Michigan, which followed South Carolina by

three days. One of the things people forecast was that we were going to win South Carolina and therefore get a bounce in Michigan. I always thought that Michigan was going to be difficult for us, because what happened in South Carolina really stayed in South Carolina. We hadn't rehabilitated ourselves nationally against McCain, and thus we were still weak in Michigan.

We lost it, and it was very difficult after we lost Michigan.

Washington and Virginia were the real Super Tuesday. The race was won not on Super Tuesday with California, New York, and Ohio, but a week after Michigan when we carried Washington. I think Washington was the pivotal point when McCain was basically done. I think his planners made a big mistake by doing what they did in Virginia, and not competing as strongly in Washington. I felt Washington was a perfect state for a McCain-type candidacy. They had raised expectations in Washington by saying, "We may lose the Republican vote, but we're going to win the popular vote." They ended up losing both. I think it was crucial. On March 7 we won it. We won most of the states in which we competed. Then on March 14 we clinched it.

After the primaries were over, we were dead even with Gore. A lot of people say Bush was ahead, and he had a 15- or 20-point lead. But the race was roughly tied when the primaries were over in mid-March. Then, for four or six weeks, the campaign made a concerted effort to have policy initiatives every week. Bush laid out what he was going to do on various policies: Social Security, all the different things. Bush had new ideas. I think that four- or six-week period was crucial, because in that period of time, we went from even to about 6 points up.

I think the effect of it was that it stopped all the Washington talk and the press talk like "Look, these guys had all this lead, they raised $75 million at the time, what happened to it all? What are they doing?" Doing what we did and getting the poll numbers back up to 5 or 6 points stopped a lot of that chatter and said the Bush campaign really knows what it's doing. Everybody backed off about who needed to be fired. We went through "who needs to be fired" a number of different times. After New Hampshire, who needs to be fired? After the primaries are over, who needs to be fired? To give the President credit, he never bought into any of that. He really stuck to the team and stayed with the team.

The other thing that happened in the same period of time was one of the first instances of Gore reinforcing a negative preconception. People forget that the Elian Gonzalez announcement was on March 30 or March 29, when Gore said, "I'm going to go against the President on this and I'm going to do this, and I'm going to make my announcement." Even though Gore said, "Well, I previously said this in November of '99," it reinforced the perception that Gore would do things for political reasons, not for the right reason. Whether it was true or not, it was the perception of a lot of voters, and the Elian announcement reinforced it and helped us during that four- or six-week policy initiative. It got us back on our feet and up in the polls.

Everybody here at the school has probably talked about early paid media effects and the ramifications. There's been a lot of discussion about the June–July period, when the Democratic National Committee spent about $30 million. One thing that happened was that many people bought into the Dick Morris theory from 1996. According to that theory, early media changed the race against Bob Dole, basically taking the race from close to a big lead, and that's when the race was won or lost. I believe that is an urban political legend. If you look at the poll numbers before the advertising and after the advertising, they actually went from 16 or 17 down nationally before the media started to 12 down nationally when the media was over.

What decided the 1996 race was the government shutdown, with Forbes attacking Dole every day leading up to the primary. The other thing was that Clinton's job approval ratings were good. The country had a decent right track/wrong track assessment in polls, and the voters were basically in the position to re-elect the President.

What was crucial in 2000 was the fact that the Democratic National Committee outspent us by $10 million in the summer. In the end, if you total it all, with the amount of money that the DNC/Gore and the amount of money RNC/Bush had to spend on media, they were roughly at parity with one exception, the California Republican Party's media.

Take out the California Republican Party media and we spent about the same amount of money. We had $10 million more to spend in the final month of the campaign because we didn't compete with the Democrats in the summer on the media.

In the end, the facts bear out that when their summer advertising was finished and our convention was finished, we were 14 or 15 points up. We started the summer 6 or 7 up. The advertising happened. Somebody could argue that in that time their advertising affected the race. We never saw it in our poll numbers in any other states, but in the end the conventions happened, and we got our bounce and were back up 15. So it was like the advertising never happened.

If I had to do it over again I would have argued basically not to spend anything in the summer time. The problem is that it's very difficult to sustain that argument if somebody else is spending $30 million and you're not spending any money. Everybody thinks you're crazy if you don't spend your own money. But if I had to do it over again, I would argue strenuously not to do spending in a similar circumstance.

The conventions. We received the bounce we thought we were going to get. The convention ran very well. Gore got the bounce we thought he would. Gore actually had two bounces. He had the Lieberman preconvention bounce; when he picked Joe Lieberman he got a bounce that didn't go away or settle out. Then he had a bounce from the final two days of his convention. From what we looked at, the first two days really didn't add anything to the Gore effort, but the final two days did. When it was over, the race was roughly even.

Then we started trending down in the period I call the Fields of September. Mark McKinnon refers to it as the month of "rats, moles, and bad polls." September was a horrible month. We had this great convention; everybody thought we were 15 points up, and then all of a sudden the Democrats pick Lieberman and have their convention and the lead was gone. The race was dead even.

We were behind in September. We weren't behind before Labor Day, but we were behind in the mid-September time period. A lot of things happened that changed this, but another preconception Gore reinforced involved his announcement about the Strategic Petroleum Reserve. People thought the announcement was political and not substantive. It didn't have a huge effect, but it did have some effect. What really got us the race, instead of us turning downward and losing it for us by 5 or 6 or 7 points, were the debates.

In the first two debates Gore again confirmed a preconception people had. In focus groups and polls, people thought he wasn't a nice person (I actually believe he is; he's a decent person and actually a funny person, if you know him, I guess), that he lectured and that he did things for political reasons. He confirmed all three of those things in the first two debates. He made pronouncements that indicated that he was willing to say or do anything politically. His "sighs" and bearing made him look like he wasn't a nice person, and at points, when he answered questions, he lectured. He actually did more damage to himself than we did to him. We helped ourselves by combating the preconceptions that Bush was in over his head, that he didn't know what he was doing, he couldn't stand up against Gore in a debate, and that he really wasn't ready. We combated all these.

Gore had more of a negative effect on himself than we had a positive effect on ourselves. A year and a half before, had anyone said, "The debates are really necessary. The debates are going to get you back on track," we would've all laughed.

The other thing that people often miss is the effect of the Cheney/Lieberman debate. We had a bump after the Cheney/Lieberman debate. Cheney was widely viewed as having won it. People really liked the guy. They liked the fact that he was on the ticket and that he was going to be in the White House. The vice presidential debate, which normally doesn't have much impact, helped us.

Turnout. I have to give the Democrats a lot of credit for what they did in the final four days—what they did among African Americans and union members and in certain states among Hispanics. These groups exceeded the normal percentage they contribute on Election Day. They did an unbelievable job. Turnout was part of the reason this race went from one we thought we were going to win by 3 points a week out to one that was roughly even.

I'm sure there are going to be questions about the impact of the DUI, which I'll be happy to answer. I still don't think anybody has a clear idea how much effect releasing that information the Thursday before the election had. Turnout was the biggest factor. I think conservatives were down as a percentage of the vote. To a large degree, the Democratic base was up over what you'd normally see.

The other thing that happened on Election Day was that late deciders, who normally go with challengers, broke toward the Vice President. To a large degree it was because the late deciders had a huge right track/wrong track advantage. They were much more solid for Gore, because they felt the country was on the right track rather than on the wrong track. In some surveys it was plus 50. That differential all along worked against us, but especially the last weekend.

There's a lot of discussion about issues versus personality, that Gore had the issues and Bush had the personality, and personality won. I personally don't believe either one of those things affects how elections are decided. Issues and personality are signals of broader values Americans hold. People see a candidate's stand on issues as a sign of whether he understands their problems: "Does he care about me? Is he ready to lead?" Those things determine how elections are decided, not, "I like this guy."

Liking takes you to "Is this guy like me? Am I comfortable with this person? Am I ready for this person to lead the country?" I don't think people make their decisions on voting based on issues or personality. These are signals of broader values. If people decided elections based on issues, Jimmy Carter would have won in 1980. He would have beaten Ronald Reagan. If you polled on every issue and said, "Here's Carter's position, here's Reagan's position," the vast majority of the public thought Carter had the right position on the issues. I don't think voters have a litmus test where they say, "Okay, Bush. We got Bush on tax cuts, and we got Social Security. Okay, Gore, Bush; Gore, Bush. Okay, eight Gore, two Bush. I'm going to vote for Gore." They don't vote that way. Again, issues and personality are signals toward broader values.

Finally, campaign effects versus historical models. There's been a lot of discussion since Election Day by a lot of political scientists who predicted that Gore would get somewhere between 53 and 60 percent in a two-way race. It obviously didn't happen that way. There were a couple of reasons why. One, campaigns matter! As you've seen in some of the postelection analysis by these same political scientists who didn't believe campaigns matter, their argument now is that Gore didn't get 53 or 60 percent of the vote because he ran a bad campaign. Well, their whole theory was premised on the fact that campaigns don't matter, but now they're basically arguing that Gore and his team ran a bad campaign. I actually thought they ran a pretty good campaign. Campaigns matter. They don't matter in a huge spectrum, they matter on the margins. I believe long-term factors and campaign effects operate simultaneously. Historical models to a large degree describe the playing field you play on. In some cases those factors will determine the presidential result. Campaigns can affect the result on a 4 or 5 percent range, which obviously in this election had a big impact.

Political scientists miss one thing, and I think it's because they don't have the data going back enough years to judge it. They took Clinton's job approval rating, and obviously they took the right track/wrong track question, and I don't know the model they put it through, but they put it through one and it came out with 53 percent. They didn't factor in the fact that, though Clinton had a high job approval rating, his personal favorability was the exact opposite of his job approval rating. Normally, a president's job approval rating and personal favorability rating are roughly the same. If you look at the polls today, Bush has a little higher personal favorability than he does job approval rating. But they're usually at rough parity. Clinton's weren't that way. Clinton had a high job approval rating and a low personal favorability. When they premised the model on job approval rating without taking into account this personal favorability, which basically said, "It's time for a change because we're tired of the moral values and all that stuff," they missed that calculation. Again, it's partially because they don't have enough data going back in the presidential years to put in personal favorability, but if they had looked at the two sides with arrows for Clinton going both ways, I don't think their models would have come out with a 60 percent Gore victory.

FRED STEEPER. I want to deal with a couple of issues in the campaign where the campaigns had different messages, possibly because they were interpreting public opinion differently. One was the Social Security issue and the other the gun control issue.

The Social Security issue in particular fascinated me because neither campaign really backed off on that issue, and it was as though the two campaigns were looking at different data. So I wanted to go through what we were seeing and how we were interpreting it, and why we felt we had the right message on it. It would be interesting, as the Democrat consultants come forward later, to see how they were viewing it.

Fred Steeper. Photo by Kyle Cassidy.

Very early in April 1999, in a Republican National Committee poll, we just measured the base, the simple idea of allowing people to invest a portion of their taxes in their own investment retirement accounts. You could see that the results were overwhelmingly in favor of this.

When you give people a categorical position, you often get an inflated degree of support. A stiffer test is to pit it against some alternatives. At the time, the Clinton administration was advocating that a portion of Social Security tax dollars should be invested in the private markets, but that the government should do it. We tested the first idea against the Clinton administration's position at the time, and also put in the third alternative, which was important, to raise and remind people of whatever attitudes they

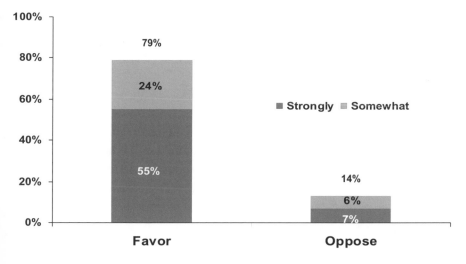

BASIC IDEA OF INDIVIDUAL INVESTMENT
"Let people put a portion of their Social Security payroll taxes into their own retirement investment accounts."

U.S. National Survey April 1999

INDIVIDUAL INVESTMENT AND TWO ALTERNATIVES
"Which one of these three policies do you most favor for Social Security?"

Let *people* put a portion of their Social Security payroll taxes into their own retirement investment accounts.	**61%**
Have the *federal government* invest a portion of people's Social Security payroll taxes in retirement investment accounts.	**20%**
Do *not allow* any social security payroll taxes to be invested in the *stock market*.	**14%**

U.S. National Survey, May 1999

had about the risk in the stock market. That was the reason for the third alternative.

The results were overwhelmingly in favor of giving people control over part of their Social Security taxes. In other research on this, there's a great deal of cynicism about the federal government being able to do anything right, which translated to the federal government not having the ability to properly invest people's Social Security dollars.

Even with overall support for this new idea, this reform in Social Security, there was a concern, politically, as to how different

AGE GROUP REACTIONS

"Which one of these three policies do you most favor for Social Security?"

	Age Groups			
	18-24	25-39	40-64	65+
Let *people put a portion* of their Social Security payroll taxes into their own retirement investment accounts.	71%	70%	63%	40%
Have the *federal government* invest a portion of people's Social Security payroll taxes in retirement investment accounts.	18	17	20	24
Do *not allow* any social security payroll taxes to be invested in the *stock market*.	11	9	13	24

U.S. National Survey, May 1999

age groups feel, and whether this is something that senior citizens would be against. You do see the expected age pattern. The younger voters are overwhelmingly in favor of having this new choice. It drops off with seniors, but not to the extent that now it makes it politically a big error in terms of winning the senior citizen vote. Forty percent of seniors are actually going for this new reform. Twenty-four percent are saying that none of the Social Security dollars should go into the private marketplace, but it's only 24 percent.

We collected these data in early 1999. In the Bush polling,

what we often did was take what the candidates were actually saying about the issues, the rhetoric, the terms, how they were framing the issues, and read them to our survey respondents. These are the words that the Bush campaign was choosing to use to describe their position on Social Security, and then the Gore campaign's position on Social Security.

We presented these in a survey, and asked people, given that the candidates are saying these very different things about Social Security, does it make you more likely to vote for Bush, or more likely to vote for Gore? We asked this particular question in a couple key swing states. While the margin in favor of having the ability to personally invest your own Social Security dropped, it was still above 50 percent.

BUSH PROPOSAL v. GORE PROPOSAL

BUSH proposes a *bipartisan* plan that *guarantees* everyone at or near retirement *every penny* of their benefits. *No cuts* in Social Security. Plan gives taxpayers *choice* to invest a *small part* of their Social Security in sound investments they *control* for *higher* returns.

GORE proposes to *pay off the national debt* and put the money that would have gone into interest payments into Social Security; he would build on the Social Security base with a *new retirement savings account* with the *government matching* the savings for *low and middle* income families.

Statewide Surveys, June, 2000

But this result was very encouraging. Even against the competitive message of the Gore campaign, the Bush message clearly
had the majority in favor of it. We also tested this idea using
Gore's attack on the Bush plan. At one time he used the term
"Wall Street roulette," and tried to engender the fear that the proposal was much too risky. We pitted those against each other and
again the Bush proposition won out by a 50 to 38 percent margin.
These were the kind of data we were looking at.

There has been a change in people's perceptions of Social Security. There are more investors now with experience investing
their own money. I think that has changed public opinion over the
last two or two or three decades. This is really an idea whose time
has come. There is substantial support for it. But right to the end,

BUSH PROPOSAL v. GORE PROPOSAL

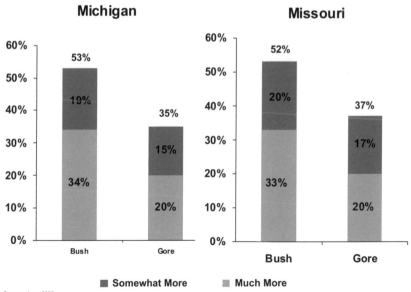

Statewide Surveys, June, 2000

BUSH PROPOSAL / GORE ATTACK

BUSH proposes a *bipartisan* plan that *guarantees* everyone at or near retirement *every penny* of their benefits. *No cuts* in Social Security. Plan gives taxpayers *choice* to invest a *small part* of their Social Security in sound investments they   *control* for *higher* returns.   50%

GORE says Bush's proposal to divert Social Security taxes to the stock market is playing *Wall Street Roulette* with the nation's retirement program. By *diverting* money into *private* accounts, his scheme would lead to   *bankruptcy* and *break the contract* of guaranteed benefits.   38%

Multi-State Survey, June 2000

the Gore campaign critiqued our position on this, saying that we had too risky a scheme, and that this was going to undermine Social Security. This was an asset and an offensive issue for them, whereas the data we were looking at gave us the impression that we had a good, solid message.

Regarding both Social Security and gun control, I think it was assumed that the Republicans and the Bush campaign were on the short side of public opinion. But the way we measured the issue, we didn't think that was the case on Social Security. A lot of early polls over the past decade have shown a substantial majority of people supporting restrictions on the sale of guns. But take that position and pit it against an alternative position, for ex-

ENFORCEMENT V. RESTRICTIONS ON SALES

*"Which one of these two actions to reduce gun violence
do you think would do the most good?"*

	All	Cons. Rep.	Swing Voters	Lib. Dem.
Mandatory jail time for those who commit a crime with a gun.	58%	72%	55%	48%
Greater restrictions on the sale of guns.	33	22	34	47

U.S. National Survey, April 1999

ample: Which would be a more effective way of reducing gun violence in America, greater restrictions on the sale of guns, or having mandatory jail time for those who commit a crime? Here we find an alternative that people think would be more effective than general restrictions on gun sales.

In a campaign, what you're looking for is something with solid support from your own base but also majority support from swing voters. In this case, 47 percent of the liberal Democrats are saying greater restrictions on guns, but 48 percent are saying that, given the above choice, they would go for mandatory jail time.

We worded this question in early 1999 as a hypothetical trial heat between a Republican for Congress and a Democrat for

Congress. Here we're inserting the important concept of the necessity of more vigorous enforcement of current gun control laws, which you heard about later on in the 2000 campaign. That produced a spread of 70 to 25 percent. It was clearly very popular with the Republican conservative base and 69 percent of the swing voters, so right there you've got, politically, a very good position on gun control. What we really learned here is that there are other forms of gun control. Enforcing existing laws is a type of gun control. Actually, the public perceives it as being more effective than restrictions on the general sales.

In the Bush polling we often like to present the positions of the two campaigns in their own words. The Gore attack on Bush's position on gun control stated that his position was dictated by the NRA, that he was in favor of concealed weapons, and that he

ENFORCEMENT V. RESTRICTIONS ON SALES
"Which one of these two candidates for Congress are you more likely to vote for, based just on this information?"

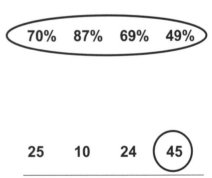

	All	Cons. Rep.	Swing Voters	Lib. Dem.
A *REPUBLICAN* who voted in favor of more vigorous *enforcement* of existing gun control laws and *mandatory penalties* for criminals who use a gun.	70%	87%	69%	49%
A *DEMOCRAT* who voted in favor of greater *restrictions on the sale* of guns to the general public.	25	10	24	45

May 1999

allowed weapons in the churches. That's a very strong attack, and one that we were anticipating. We put that against Bush critiquing the Clinton administration for not enforcing current gun control laws.

We got a rather surprising result when we first measured it, but clearly by 65 to 29 the emphasis on enforcement of current laws outweighed this attack on Bush's position as being too permissive regarding gun rights.

We took this idea to a few key states. We changed the wording somewhat, but it was the same Gore attack on Bush's position. Here we've tightened up the Bush position a little more and put more emphasis on supporting tougher penalties and enforcement of gun laws.

We measured this in three different states, and the results we

GORE ATTACK / BUSH ENFORCEMENT

GORE says Bush's priorities on gun control are *dictated by the NRA* . Bush, as Texas Governor, made it possible for the first time in 125 years for private citizens to carry *concealed weapons* , made it easier to carry guns to *church*, limited the ability of cities to *sue gun makers* , and now Bush opposes mandatory *child safety locks* .

BUSH says the Clinton-Gore Administration *failed to enforce existing* gun control laws. They have *prosecuted only 13 students* under federal law for possessing a firearm in a school zone, though 3,930 were expelled for doing so. Overall gun *prosecutions have dropped 46%* under Clinton-Gore. Bush *supports tougher penalties* for crimes committed with guns, *more prosecutors* to enforce gun laws, and *background checks* at gun shows to keep guns away from children and criminals.

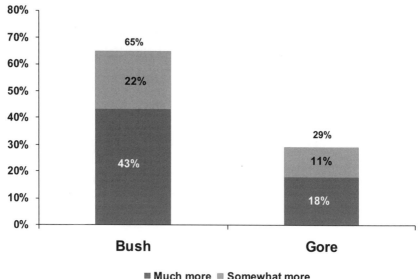

GORE ATTACK / BUSH ENFORCEMENT

Multi-State Survey, April 2000

■ **Much more** ■ **Somewhat more**

got aren't the same from state to state. There isn't much of a pro-gun sentiment in Illinois, but even in Illinois the Bush position came out ahead 49 to 40, and in the key states of Michigan and Missouri you could see that this position of more emphasis on tougher laws and enforcing the current laws clearly has the majority support.

On both on Social Security and gun control, the feeling was that we were vulnerable, but we learned something about public opinion in both instances. There was clear public support for a new reform, and there was an alternative to general new restrictions on gun sales. There was substantial support for enforcing

GORE ATTACK / BUSH ENFORCEMENT

GORE says Bush's priorities on gun control are *dictated by the NRA* . Bush, as Texas Governor, made it possible for the first time in 125 years for private citizens to carry *concealed weapons* , made it easier to carry guns to *church*, limited the ability of cities to *sue gun makers* , and now Bush opposes mandatory *child safety locks* .

BUSH says we need to *hold criminals responsible* for their actions, and the *Clinton Gore* Administration has *failed to enforce existing* gun control laws. Of 3900 violators caught with guns in school zones, the Clinton-Gore Administration has prosecuted only 13. *Bush supports tougher penalties* for crimes committed with guns and *more prosecutors* to enforce gun laws.

Statewide Surveys, May, June 2000

current laws, and that, politically, turned out to be the right message to give in the campaign, on two issues that were commonly thought to be vulnerabilities for us.

Campaigns are as much about personal qualities as issues. Matthew Dowd said that none of these are really important, and he may be absolutely right. People may take their perceptions, their personal qualities and issues, and make an overall judgment about the two candidates. But to the extent that some voters are using individual perceptions, I thought I'd show you a way to summarize the difference of varied perceptions people have had in their heads about these two candidates. We looked at 13 personality qualities, of which we thought seven were important in this campaign. You may be able to think of others, but either they are redundant, or we tried them and they just didn't make the correlation cut.

We performed several types of correlation analyses to see how these were affecting people's voting decision. The first three— "shares your values," "ready to handle the job," and "truthful"— had the highest impact. The next two ("strong leader" and "cares about people's problems") had substantial impact; the last two ("likeable" and "has new ideas") had an independent impact, but not as much as the others. Bush had the advantage on three of these: truthful, strong leader, and has new ideas. He consistently

GORE ATTACK / BUSH ENFORCEMENT

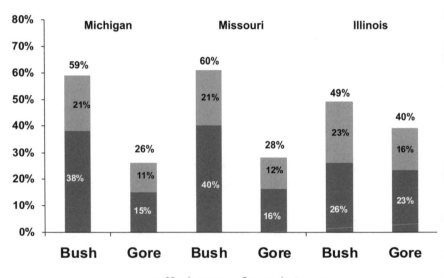

Statewide Surveys, May, June 2000

had the advantage on those three whether he was ahead or behind on the polls.

Those were three strong points for him. Gore always had the lead on cares about people's problems, but that's tapping into a bias that people bring into any campaign. We're going to assume that the compassion element is more a Democratic attribute.

The other six qualities really don't carry a party bias. It's important that of those six, Bush was consistently ahead on three. The two I have labeled "mixed" depend on who was ahead in the trial heat. People tend to move their perceptions into line with one another to support their voting choice. So in that period when Bush did fall behind, after the Democratic convention through

VOTE DRIVERS: Issues and Personal Qualities

	Correlation	Advantage
Shares Your Values	Very High	Tie
Ready to Handle Job	Very High	Mixed
Truthful	Very High	Bush
Strong Leader	High	Bush
Education	High	"Gore"
Moral Values	High	Bush
Taxes	High	Bush
Economy	High	Mixed
Cares About People's Problems	High	Gore
Health Care	High	Gore
Social Security	High	Tie
Likeable	Moderate	Mixed
Has New Ideas	Moderate	Bush

the first weeks of September, Gore did go ahead on "ready to handle the job" and on "likeable." When Bush was ahead or tied, he was ahead on "likeable" and on "ready to handle the job."

I'd be interested to know whether the Democrats ever even put "shares your values" on their list. I think that's a very important quality opposed to the view of voting as pocketbook issues, a materialistic interpretation of voting. It's almost common lore that the most important thing are people's pocketbooks.

What I find in research is that it's really much more important, or elections are much more about, finding the candidate who "shares my values" as opposed to the candidate who's going to pass a program that's somehow is going to benefit me materially. Sure enough, when we run these correlation analyses, the candidate chosen as "shares my values" always has an extremely high correlation with vote preference, controlling for everything else in a model.

We also monitored who was preferred on the issues the voters thought were most important. The six most important issues in this campaign taken individually were education, moral values, taxes, the economy, health care, and Social Security. Those were at the top of the issue agenda.

I put Gore in quotation marks on education, because he did consistently have a lead, but it was a single-digit lead, which we took as being encouraging, because this typically is an issue that the Democratic party has owned. That single digit indicated that we were making some progress, and were making our points on the education issue. But to the extent that voters are playing with different perceptions, different individual estimates of the candidates, we were finding we couldn't discard any of these 13. They kept showing in our multiple correlation analysis as having impact on the vote.

Five of these are Bush advantages, three favor Gore, two are tied, and three are mixed depending on what time we were in the election.

To the extent that voters were making their decisions based on this calculation, they had a number of things they were trying to consider. It was clear that neither candidate had the overwhelming advantage across these 13. By looking at these data, you could see that the election was going to be very close.

KATHY SOSA (Garcia LKS). I'm just wondering whether either of you have an answer to why it would be mixed on the economy. Wouldn't you expect Gore to be the clear leader on the economy?

Matthew Dowd and Fred Steeper. Photo by Kyle Cassidy.

What was it that led to this being even? We were in a great economy, and things were going really well—better than anybody can remember. How did that happen?

DOWD. I think that one of the misperceptions the press had was that if the economy was good, Gore would benefit automatically and get the credit for it, and people would perceive that Gore would somehow do a better job than Bush on it. If you go back and look historically at that question, they've asked that in Gallup polls. At times when the economy was good, it didn't necessarily mean that the person representing that economy led on the attribute "Who could handle the economy better?" That's another example of a judgment people make related to leadership. Just because the economy's good doesn't mean that they conclude that Gore could handle the economy better. He did have it going for him, but the fact that we always led on strong leadership countered that.

But historically, because the economy's good doesn't mean that the person running for reelection is credited with that. It has to do with leadership. Kennedy/Nixon is a perfect example. The economy was turning around in 1960. Kennedy always led on who could handle the economy in the 1960 polls even though Nixon was the incumbent vice president and the economy was turning around.

KARLYN CAMPBELL (University of Minnesota). The polls just before the election suggested that Bush was going to win the popular vote. He didn't. What kind of data do you have about the issues that made a difference in late deciders in that final period that might explain why those polls were wrong?

DOWD. I think that most of the polls were right, if you look at them. Most of the polls showed a closing in the final weekend.

Some people just stopped polling the Thursday before. But most of them showed this race being very tight in the end. Our polls showed the race being very tight in the end.

Two things happened. One was the turnout mechanism. The Democrats ran a much closer race than we initially thought. Between Thursday and Tuesday, we asked the question, "Regardless of whom you are going to vote for, who do you think is going to win?" This, in our view, is an important question—not so much for what you learn, and how you're going to act as a result, but how you're going to do among the undecideds. If you lead on that question among undecided voters, in the end you're more apt to get those voters than people who think you're not going to win. It's what people call the bandwagon effect. It's not huge, but it is there. Bush had been growing on that ever since the debates. After that it sort of settled out. We led on that issue by 10 or 12 points. Even among Democrats there were 20 or 25 percent who thought we were going to win the election.

That number began to close after the Thursday before the election. The margin in vote preference was still roughly 3 or 4, but "Who do you think is going to win the election?" closed. It started closing on Friday, Saturday, Sunday, and Monday. To a degree, that affected turnout. It affected Democratic turnout up and it affected conservative turnout down. In the end, it made a difference. Coupled with the turnout mechanism, the Democrats had roughly 3 points. But most of the public polls that kept polling were right. They basically called the race a tie—1 or 2 points.

KATHLEEN FRANKOVIC (CBS News). Bob Erickson, who's a professor at Columbia University, was modeling the impact of the possibility of a tie vote on the Electoral College and what would be necessary to win the Electoral College. Based on all the public polls state by state, he told me that his judgment about what happened in the final days was that all the movement toward Gore took place in those states that were not the battleground states. Essentially the impact of the change on a national level was measurable, but it was concentrated in the states where there'd been little advertising, where the public might not have focused on the campaigns. So you had increasing leads in places such as California, New York, New Jersey, Massachusetts, Illinois, et cetera, and that actually in the battleground states there wasn't this sort of shift. Do you have any insight into that?

STEEPER. In the battleground states the race looked extremely close even before the last weekend. It did seem, from the state and national polling, that the two weren't in synch. The national polling was indicating a clear Bush victory of 4 or 5 points before that last weekend. But looking at the battleground state polling during that week, it was still problematic as who was going to win the race. So it may be absolutely right that Gore gained more in the nonbattleground states, whereas the battleground polling all along was showing that the race was going to be very tight in terms of states that could swing their electoral votes either way.

DOWD. The first thing that happened is we didn't carry Texas by as much as we had thought. We lost California and New York by a lot more. That's why we never envisioned a scenario where Gore would win the popular vote and lose the Electoral College. In the summer of '99, I put out a memo that said it was a distinct but not sure possibility that we could win the popular vote and lose the Electoral College. The memo was premised on the fact that we'd have a huge margin in Texas and other states in the south, and we wouldn't be as far apart in New York and California. We could win the popular vote by 500,000 to 600,000 votes, and lose the Electoral College. I never envisioned a scenario where the reverse would happen, because I thought we'd come out with huge margins in those other places.

ELIHU KATZ (University of Pennsylvania). It seems to me that your explanation is all based on the national vote. But Bush lost the national vote. Now you're talking about the states' vote, which seems to be the crucial thing that's been omitted in the exposition.

DOWD. No, states were the crucial thing. We never put together a plan to win the popular vote. We put together a plan in the states that we targeted based on winning the electoral college vote. Just so you know, we never conducted a national poll after December 1999.

STEEPER. Much of that information I was showing you was based on polling twenty swing states. I actually never showed a national number because there are so many national numbers you can get for free. Our polling was in twenty swing states. I was showing you either a specific state or a representative sample of what we considered the twenty swing states.

DOWD. Which, to be honest, was a big topic for internal discussion in the campaign: that we weren't going to poll nationally, we were going to pick the twenty states we thought were the battleground, and only poll in individual states or as a group. But we didn't do a national poll after December of '99.

HENRY KENSKI (University of Arizona). I'd like to ask a question about advertising. You mentioned that Gore got the postconvention bounce. After Labor Day, up until about September 20, Gore had moved ahead. One theory why he went ahead was the media theory, the smooch theory, and the convention. Another is—and this is the point of information I'd like clarified—that the Bush campaign went dark, it is alleged, and didn't really advertise in the seventeen battleground states for a period of two or three weeks. That's one thing I had read. Did you cut back, or did you not advertise much in September, and could Gore's emergence be attributed to heavier advertising than you did in those three weeks in September?

DOWD. We went on the air the weekend or the Monday after the Democratic Convention and never went off.

STEEPER. That was also a bad period in terms of the news, not only positive for Gore but negative for Bush. That was the period of some stumbles on the part of the campaign. Rather than the Bush campaign getting the message out during those three weeks, we kept getting thrown off because of various mistakes, and didn't get back in line until the third week in September. It was a combination of a very good Gore campaign and a Bush campaign that probably had its worst period of the general election cycle.

Which is to say it was free media-driven rather than driven by advertising.

CURTIS GANS (Committee for the Study of the American Electorate). You mentioned that you profited because McCain put so many resources in Virginia. It strikes me that you may have profited by three other mistakes. One was McCain going into South Carolina at all. That was a targeting mistake. The other is that the Gore campaign, based on the results, didn't target Ohio, which ended up a lot closer than anybody realized. Third, you benefited from network coverage on the Virginia/Washington night. They quickly declared Bush a winner in Washington. He ended up winning with 2,307 votes with 40 percent absentee after a week of counting. It would've given a whole different perception to Super Tuesday if you were not perceived as the clear winner in Washington.

DOWD. I do believe that McCain had an opportunity to win South Carolina, so I don't think it was a mistake running there. I think he made a mistake in South Carolina when he talked about George Bush being like Bill Clinton. When he put up that spot, our numbers went up and, when we put up our spot reacting to that spot, which I think was called "Integrity," our numbers moved.

We put that spot up in other states that hadn't even seen the McCain spot, and our numbers moved. That was a big mistake when he put that spot on the air in South Carolina. I think he did compete in Ohio. He put advertising on the air in Ohio. But he didn't put as much. I agree with you, he could have done a better job in Ohio.

I completely agree with you about Washington and Virginia. Because Washington was a later time zone, and the networks wanted to call the day early, it's actually another example of calling it and then afterward finding it a lot closer than they originally assumed. This is what happened on November 7. It happened a little earlier in the calendar, but I agree with you. We had a huge benefit from the fact they called it.

Two

Carter Eskew
and Bob Shrum

Carter Eskew's links with Vice President Al Gore stretch back to the early 1970s. Having graduated from Exeter, Yale, and Columbia, Mr. Eskew spent two summers as a reporter at the Nashville Tennessean, *where his desk was next to Mr. Gore's. Mr. Eskew is formerly a partner in the media firm of Grunwald, Eskew, Donilon and earlier Squier Eskew. In 1995, he chose to work with BSMG worldwide, and became president of Bozell/Eskew, working on the campaigns of corporate giants including Microsoft. During the 2000 presidential campaign, he was one of Al Gore's closest advisers, serving as senior strategist in charge of the message team.*

Bob Shrum began his career in politics as the principal speechwriter to Senator George McGovern in the 1972 Democratic campaign for president. He subsequently served as staff director and chief counsel to the United States Senate Select Committee on Nutrition and Human Needs, and as press secretary and speechwriter to Senator Edward Kennedy. Since 1985, Mr. Shrum has produced advertisements for twenty-seven winning U.S. Senate campaigns, for six governors, the mayors of

New York, Los Angeles, Chicago, Philadelphia, Denver, Dade County, and San Francisco, as well as the speaker and the Democratic leader of the U.S. House of Representatives. He is now chairman of the political media-consulting firm Shrum, Devine and Donilon. Mr. Shrum was a fellow at the Kennedy School of Government at Harvard University and has taught at Yale and Boston College. As a journalist, his work has appeared in New York Magazine, Los Angeles Times, New York Times, *and the* New Republic. *During the 2000 campaign, Mr. Shrum was senior adviser to Vice President Al Gore during his successful campaign for the Democratic nomination and a senior adviser to the Gore/Lieberman 2000 campaign.*

BOB SHRUM. The *Washington Post* had a little story on the historians who wanted to explain how, having engaged in an extraordinary degree of social science hubris using a case study based on ten or twelve presidential elections, they could have been wrong in predicting an Al Gore victory. One said the economy was not as important as the models had assumed. Another said that Gore didn't run enough on the economy. Another said Gore lost because he didn't run close enough to Clinton. Another said it was because of the Clinton scandals. No one said Bush ran a good campaign, although we believe that to be true. And then of course there was one historian who said, wait a minute, Gore won.

The models were right and the exit polls were right. What we're going to do today is not refight this battle but try to describe, from what we obviously understand is an aligned perspective, what we saw during the 2000 campaign and why it happened.

At the outset let me make a personal note. I'm amazed that some people in the Democratic Party think that the most useful thing to do now is examine why Gore "lost" instead of focusing on the fact that he won, that he won more votes than George W.

Bush, more votes than any other Democrat ever, and more votes than Clinton ever did. And he did it in the face of a third party challenge on the left, not the right, which is what helped President Clinton to victory, in 1992 especially. We did make mistakes. We're going to try and talk about them.

Bob Shrum. Photo by Kyle Cassidy.

The Bush people did run a very effective campaign, but to suggest, as for example the Democratic Leadership Council does, on the basis of polling by Mark Penn—who's a good friend of mine, and whom I respect, but with whom I disagree—that this was an easy election, and Al Gore should've easily won it, ignores two salient realities.

First, early on, when Mark was the chief pollster for the campaign, moving it along the lines he recommends, Al Gore was losing to George W. Bush in the summer of 1999 by margins of 14 to 18 percent. Second are the data that this analysis omits, and the polling doesn't even investigate in depth: the problems presented by the President's personal approval ratings, especially among soft and undecided voters in battleground states. The resulting disadvantage I think Al Gore faced was on the values dimensions, which determined so much of voter choice in 2000.

I defended President Clinton. So did most of us during the assault against him. I would do it again, and I would do it proudly. But does anyone doubt the plain fact that if there had been no so-called scandals, and we had the economy we did have in 2000, who would be sitting in the Oval Office today?

So what Carter and I will do this morning is look back and analyze what we thought were the genuinely complicated challenges that the Gore campaign faced, and how the campaign dealt or failed to deal with them. One last preliminary note: Carter came to the campaign in July 1999. In many ways, aside from the candidate, I believe he was the heart and spirit of the campaign. He had an enormous effect on it. He helped bring me and others into the campaign after that, including my partner, Tad Devine, who ultimately played a critical role that we'll talk about later. At the time that Carter came, and shortly after I came, the Vice President looked as if he might very well lose the nomination to Senator Bradley. We want to look back on what happened from then on.

Carter Eskew. Photo by Kyle Cassidy.

CARTER ESKEW. I think it's important to start a discussion of the race at least understanding our perspective; we actually believe that we won the election. We won the popular vote by more than 500,000. We think we won the Electoral College as well. The *Miami Herald* analysis in December, which I frankly didn't look at too closely, seemed to indicate that a fair accounting of the votes would produce a Gore margin. Our sense in the Gore campaign is that a fair counting of the votes would have led to an Electoral College victory as well. It's also important to remember that within that popular vote margin are some interesting things that underlie it.

First of all, we won every Democratic primary and caucus, despite the fact that we were outspent on television. Now that is a tribute to two things: Senator Bradley's ability to raise a lot of money, and our ability to waste a lot of money early on in the process.

But the fact of the matter is, really from New Hampshire on, that—from our point of view, almost too good to be true—[there was a] period of blackout of the Democratic primary and vicious fighting on the side of the Republicans. During that period, Bradley outspent Gore considerably leading up to March 7, and also into March 14.

SHRUM. There was a critical moment that made that possible. Al Gore did something that no one ever does, no front-runner certainly ever does. He changed his campaign fundamentally in the summer. He didn't wait, like other candidates do, especially other front-runners, until he was in trouble in New Hampshire, and say "I have to do something." He changed the campaign very early on. He changed its direction, he changed its management, he changed the way it was being run.

As we went into the first debate in New Hampshire, we were actually 10 to 11 points behind in our polling there. We came out of the debate a couple of days later, 4 or 5 points, maybe 3 points behind. Most of the press had not yet caught on to that, nor to what had happened in that debate. The issues contrasts that were drawn with Bradley very early on in the primaries have a remarkable continuity—between what Gore was doing then and what he was doing in the general election. We'll show you two spots. The first, which could easily have been run in the general, and in fact at some point was, and the second, which lays down some of the issues that we were going to fight on, and that we fought on all the way through the election.

Al Gore: I know one thing very clearly about the job of president. It's the only job mentioned in the Constitution where the individual who holds that job is charged with the responsibility of fighting for all of the people, not one state, not one district, not the wealthy or the powerful or the special interests, but for all of the people, including especially those who need a voice, who need a champion, who need somebody who will lift up those who have been left behind.

Announcer: For 70 million Americans, Medicare and Medicaid are a lifeline. Al Gore: the only Democratic candidate who saves Medicare by setting aside 15 percent of the surplus to keep Medicare solvent, the only Democratic candidate who preserves Medicaid instead of replacing it with a $150 a month voucher. Al Gore: the only Democratic candidate who reforms health care in a way that protects seniors and working families. Al Gore: fighting for us.

By the way, all the spots you'll see were a cooperative effort of our firm of Carter, Mike Donilon, Tad Devine, and myself, along with Bill Knapp, who's going to talk this afternoon and who did a great job during the campaign (I hope he thinks we did, too).

ESKEW. As often was the case in the campaign, I continue to talk about things that I really know nothing about. Stan Greenberg ought to be doing this. But, as I said to you, as a personal pride section it's interesting because there's a lot of debate right now about whether the Gore campaign went too far one way or the other. The fact is, we outpolled Clinton/Gore. Gore/Lieberman outpolled Clinton/Gore in the general election among African Americans and among members of organized labor, but also did better than Clinton among Americans who make over $100,000 a year, the so-called "new economy voters." We matched Clinton's performance among suburban voters. The bottom line is that Gore received more votes than any other Democratic candidate in history, and he did it even while a third party candidate was running on the left, not the right. We believe that Gore put together a powerful winning coalition. We think this can be the new Democratic coalition. That's why we think this whole discussion is relevant. It's not just about how we defined ourselves. It's about really having a clear-eyed view of where the votes came from and what kind of coalition you have to put together as Democrats to win. It makes sense now to talk a little bit about what went right in the campaign. There's a longer section, which Bill Knapp will do, on what didn't go right in the campaign.

We can start with the message of the campaign. There's been a lot of interest in dissecting what went wrong in the campaign, and a lot of discussion about whether the Gore campaign went too far to the left and abandoned the opportunity and responsibility schematics of more centrist Democrats. I reject that.

There are two ways that I arrived at this. One is simply looking at the data to see where we actually got votes, and go back and see that we were trying to assemble a coalition with a message that had both centrist and populist elements. For example, we definitely wanted to build on the Clinton record. We embraced the notion of prosperity. But we also knew that we had to take it to the next level. So we talked about extending the prosperity, and making sure that it benefited all.

SHRUM. Stan did one critical thing, and that was help us understand that we couldn't just run on the Clinton record. We couldn't say that this election, to quote the convention speech, is "a reward for past performance." We had to make it about the future: what to do with the prosperity, especially in a situation where voters had cognitive dissonance about Clinton. We had an empirical test of running on the prosperity, in the period between the end of the primaries and when we returned to what was the primary message—and the message Al Gore was comfortable with. We ran the "prosperity and progress" or "progress and prosperity tour" in June 2000. The results were not promising. People did not respond to the idea that they were supposed to elect Al Gore for that reason. We came to this notion of the people not the powerful, fighting for working families, and fighting for families—first because it was the essence of the primary message; second, because it was what Al Gore really believed, felt, and was good at doing; and third, because fighting for working families didn't just have an economic aspect, it wasn't just about the economy.

ESKEW. We were also able to drive a values agenda of individual responsibility, the next generation of welfare reform, and tough accountability in schools. But fighting for working families was also about the more traditional fights: the patients' bill of rights, and prescription drugs.

The centrist/populist message worked together in a way that was important, but we had other goals. We had a candidate who had all the downsides of being a vice president. Also, despite the fact that most elites would grant that Gore was one of the more involved and effective vice presidents in history, the public had really no sense of that. They saw him as just a guy standing behind, not doing much. There was very little understanding of who Al Gore was. One of the things we used to say in the campaign was that both candidates were known primarily by their paternity: Bill Clinton and George Herbert Walker Bush. People brought a lot to that, both good and bad. So one of the things we needed to do with our advertising early on was to give dimension and depth and meaning to who Al Gore is, where he's from, what he cares about, what motivates him. So we did that with this bio spot, a sixty-second ad. It's always difficult to put that many eggs in a basket, but we felt it was essential. We ran it heavily in the primaries and again when we got to the general election.

Announcer: He saw his father defeated from the Senate because of his support of civil rights and gun control. And came home from Vietnam doubting politics could make a difference.

He studied religion at Vanderbilt, started a family, and worked as a reporter exposing corruption. Al Gore was only twenty-eight, but he'd seen a lot about what could go wrong in America, and decided to fight back. He won a seat in Congress and became a national leader for the environment.

He stood against the tide, opposing the Reagan budget cuts in health, education and help for the poor. As vice president, he defied the gun lobby and cast the tie-breaking vote to keep guns away from criminals. His causes: working families, improved healthcare for every American, affordable prescription drugs, revolutionary improvements in education so our test scores will be the highest in the world. A young man who decided to fight for principle is still leading the way. Al Gore: change that works for working families.

We felt Al Gore had a biography that was an advantage for us. People didn't know it. We could tell it. We felt that George Bush didn't have that same kind of biography, and in fact you never saw a real biography spot about Bush during the campaign. So we decided we would give him a biography. The way we did it was to raise doubts on the Texas record. We did this initially on the environment, before the GOP convention, because it was a place where his problem was very believable to people.

> Announcer: The issue: the environment. Al Gore has taken on big polluters to protect our air and water. The Bush plan: in Texas he appointed a chemical company lobbyist to enforce environmental laws. He made key air pollution rules voluntary, even for plants near schools. Schools now use smog meters to see if it's safe to play outside. Texas now ranks last among all states in air quality. Houston: the smog capital of the U.S. The Bush plan protects polluters instead of our families.

Then as the election moved on we moved this argument to healthcare.

> Announcer: George W. Bush says he has a plan for children's healthcare. But why hasn't he done it in Texas? Texas ranks 49th out of 50 in providing health coverage to kids. It's so bad, a federal judge just ruled Texas must take immediate corrective action. The judge's findings were that Bush's administration broke a promise to improve healthcare for kids. The needs of abused kids are neglected. Texas failed to inform families of health coverage available to a million children. The Bush record: it's becoming an issue.

At the end, we raise doubts asking "Is Bush up to the job?"

> Announcer: As governor, George W. Bush gave big oil a tax break while opposing healthcare for 220,000 kids. Texas now ranks 50th in family healthcare. He left the minimum wage at 3.35 an hour. Lets polluters police themselves. Today Texas ranks last in air quality. Now Bush promises the same $1 trillion from Social Security to two different groups. He squan-

ders the surplus on a tax cut for those making over $300,000. Is he ready to lead America?

That spot was made possible by the third debate, which I'll talk about later. At the same time, of course, our advertising was actually very heavily positive in presenting the Gore case.

I'd like to show you two spots, because they show what the heart of our advertising was. These spots ran heavily in the target states. While one of them would be considered a more centrist agenda than the other, they both worked under this rubric of fighting for families.

Announcer: Vietnam veteran. Father of four. Married 30 years. Al Gore will fight for families. Tax cuts for middle class families including a $10,000 a year tax deduction for college tuition. Continued welfare reform with time limits, work requirements. Force deadbeat parents to take responsibility for their children. A crime victims' bill of rights to protect victims, not just criminals. Fight violence and pornography on the Internet, helping parents block out what children shouldn't see. Al Gore. He'll put his values to work for us.

Al Gore: If your doctor says you need a particular specialist or some treatment, if you've got an HMO or an insurance company a lot of times some bean counter behind a computer terminal who doesn't have a license to practice medicine and doesn't have a right to play God will overrule the doctor's orders. I'm telling you, we need a patient's bill of rights to take the medical decisions away from the HMOs and insurance companies and give them back to the doctors and the nurses.

SHRUM. That was, by the way, one of the highest testing spots we ever had in a focus group. It had great power. He did it on the riverboat tour that he did after the convention. We got a number of spots out of that. They conveyed passion and gave people a very real sense of what the commitment was. Now one of the ironies was that the Gore message on what government should do for people outpolled the Bush message consistently. That was nice for us, except Bush had a really smart response. He downplayed the differences. He said he was for a patients' bill of rights. He was for a prescription drug benefit. He actually ran spots attacking us on prescription drugs. We had to respond to that, and to attacks on Social Security.

(Bush spot) Announcer: On prescription medicine, Al Gore will charge seniors a new $600 a year government access fee. George Bush opposes Gore's $600 fee. Gore's plan: when seniors turn 64 they must join a drug HMO selected by Washington or they're on their own. Bush's plan: seniors choose, and it covers all catastrophic healthcare costs. Gore's plan doesn't, and has a government HMO and a $600 fee. A prescription for disaster.

(Gore spot) Announcer: The truth about prescription drugs isn't in this notebook. It's in your checkbook. Bush relies on insurance companies. They now charge $90 a month. Under Gore, $25 a month for Medicare. Under Bush, millions of middle class seniors not covered. Under Gore, coverage available to all seniors under Medicare. Seniors choose their own doctor. Medigap still available. Under Bush, seniors forced into HMOs and insurance companies. Medicare premiums could rise 47 percent. Get all the facts.

One of the interesting things about the Bush campaign was that misleading but accurate formulation about the $600 a month. The $600 access fee came from Alex Castellanos. But one of the things that was interesting was the refusal of the Bush campaign to just cede the issue. They engaged on the issue, we reengaged. In the data, we won the issue. But we had to spend time on it. I think it was a critical issue for us in states like Florida and Pennsylvania. There was also a lot of confusion and uncertainty about Social Security. Bush had said: "Look, I'm going to preserve Social Security. You're going to have your benefit, but we're going to change it so it works for the next generation." We grappled with this over time, about how to deal with it. Then Bush gave us a great opportunity to deal with it. The spot we were able to make was very effective in the states where this whole Social Security issue was critical.

> Announcer: Is Social Security a federal program? Of course it is. But it seems George Bush doesn't understand that. Here he is talking about the Gore/Lieberman plan.
> George W. Bush: They want the federal government controlling the Social Security like it's some kind of federal program.
> Announcer: But the bigger mistake is what Bush wants to do to Social Security. Take a trillion dollars out. Promising it to young workers and seniors at the same time.
> George W. Bush: They want the federal government controlling the Social Security like it's some kind of federal program.

The argument contained in that spot, that the same trillion dollars was promised to both younger workers and seniors, was an argument we made over and over and over again. It finally really worked when we had that spot, and Bush's comment, and the third debate, where Bush couldn't explain how he promised the trillion dollars to both groups. That gives you a sense of the message interplay that we think the campaign did right up to that point.

ESKEW. We had a great convention. We needed to. We had dug

ourselves in a hole by the time we got to Los Angeles, and we needed to have a "home run." There are a lot of things that can go wrong at conventions, but we got lucky, and some things went right. The turnaround started with the selection of Joe Lieberman and the excitement that generated. I think frankly the excitement went beyond anything we in the campaign anticipated. Then Gore's speech itself, and some of the elements surrounding the speech, really gave us an opportunity to reintroduce the Vice President, giving him a fuller dimension as a person. As a result, we got the biggest postconvention bounce ever. It was real, and it was profound. It was not simply that we moved the vote to within a few points of Bush. It's all the internals that we had been struggling with. There were days when we got polls in the campaign that you really didn't want to read. You didn't want to go past the first page. These suddenly were polls you were actually looking at and smiling, because we had moved a lot of the internal dimensions on personality and character and leadership and things like that. That strength was buffeted in the rest of the campaign, but it never really left us in the way it had up until that point.

I want to say a little bit about our political strategy, for which I deserve very little credit, other than having the good sense to get some good people and let them do what they do. Under Tad Devine and Donna Brazile and Michael Whouley, we really had a very effective campaign in the target states. We were ruthless about where we spent the money. Those of you in this room who have been involved in those kinds of decisions know how difficult it can be to resist good, well-meaning people who say, "You've got to come into our state and play. If you don't, you're going to lose the race."

SHRUM. Let me let me give an example of that. Our targeting was driven almost entirely by Stan Greenberg's polling and Harrison Hickman's state-by-state polling, which told us what was going on in various states. Tad Devine was ruthless and unbending in his belief in that targeting and in his control of the money. There was a point at which we came under tremendous pressure to spend money in California. I'd be interested to know from the Bush people whether they actually believed they could win California, or whether this was an attempt to suck us in to spending a lot of money in California. I remember the day someone came in and said, "Well, there's a poll out in California that says we're only 4 points ahead. We have to go on the air in California 'cause we can't win without California." We had some contrary polling data. Tad believed in the contrary polling data. So did we, and he simply said "We will not spend money on television in California." If we had spent money on television in California, I think the election would have had a very different outcome. I think Bush would still be president, but he would have won the popular vote. But it was a critical decision to concentrate on those pure battleground states. It was also a bold decision to concentrate on Florida. It was a tough decision, and I think people at the beginning thought that it was a feint on our part, that was an attempt to draw the Bush people in.

ESKEW. That was a difficult decision because of the expense of Florida. But we did make a full-out commitment there. We were outspent considerably in Florida, but for us it was a major devotion of resources. Our campaign also closed very strongly. Everyone who knows the Vice President knows that he has this frenetic level of energy. That enabled us to cover four states in a day instead of three. The last two weeks we were only in the target states, at least once, sometimes twice. Michael Whouley had brought a team of Democratic operatives back into the fold for the final weeks of the campaign. Many of them had moved on with their lives, but decided to strap it on for one more fight. In places like Michigan and Wisconsin and Iowa and other states, we really had the best of the best. It made a huge difference in our campaign messagewise. We came to two useful things at the end. One was that the economic argument finally began to work for us. And doubts about Bush started to surface. This was inevitable. In '92, for example, when his father had been in a much weaker position, those of us who went through that campaign for Clinton can remember the race narrowing over the final days on the issue of experience. People were just starting to pause a little bit: "Is this the right decision?" I, as someone who is in the media field, want to give a lot of credit to our coordinated campaign and our field operation. They were really, really strong and good.

SHRUM. We could move strongly at the end on the economic argument. I said earlier, we couldn't run by saying, "Give me credit for the economy," but had to focus on the future economy. As we did that, voters in our polling started to give us credit for the present economy. We ran a number of economic spots. One of the most interesting things is that for all the talk of class warfare, the strategy neutralized the tax cut issue for the Republicans to the extent that Bush barely mentioned it except when asked. At the end of the race, the Bush team said the undecideds would break for the governor. In fact, they broke for Gore. We had a discussion in our own campaign about it. Undecideds, by the historic rules, break for the incumbent. Karl Rove said they were going to win by 320 electoral votes and 53 percent of the popular vote. The third debate and other factors moved the undecided vote to Gore. We won a popular vote victory almost no one except Stan Greenberg—who kept telling us every day it was possible—expected. The outcome depended on the undecided. Then of course there were people like me. I assumed we were going to win.

MARK MCKINNON (Bush campaign). We never took Florida for granted. In fact, in late August we began to get really worried about it. That Social Security ad was a direct response to what we saw happening early on in Florida. It was an early aggressive attempt to try to neutralize what we saw as an emerging advantage in Florida.

ESKEW. Some of us worked for the health care industry, the pharmaceutical industry. There's a huge body of research about how to blunt the Democratic position on the patient's bill of rights and on prescription drugs. It has to do with government control. We had a little test case in 1993 with Harry and Louise. A lot of Americans no longer think that the government is simply going to provide them with a benefit without certain costs associated with it. So I think the Bush people did exactly the right thing and did it effectively. There was a little bit of plowing that had gone on before for folks. So they were more skeptical of the claims to begin with.

SHRUM. We could answer them, but it took us a while to find the most effective answer to the $600. When we found it, we saw numbers in states like Florida moving back on prescription drugs. But I understand exactly, Mark, why you were doing what you were doing.

MCKINNON. We'd just have to neutralize that issue ultimately.

SHRUM. You did to a large extent. Instead of us winning it by 30 points, we won it by 6 points.

ESKEW. Thirteen. Stan just corrected us. We won it by 13 points.

THOMAS MANN (Brookings Institution). I'm with you in your argument with the Democratic Leadership Council about the populism and the moving left. But I wonder about the "fighting" rhetoric. Where did that came from, and what led you to embrace that in a time of prosperity? Was there an alternative to the fighting rhetoric, which seemed jarring to many of us without having the evidence presumably used in deciding on that language? The second question goes to the first debate and its impact. You probably had more to say but weren't able to. What is your impression of the understanding of the impact of the first debate on the dynamic of the race?

ESKEW. Let me answer your point about fighting. The easy answer is that we made 538 commercials and we tested every single one of them. In our case we used focus groups, dial groups, et cetera. Everything that got on the air was thoroughly researched and tested. But one of the things that people perhaps did not understand about the Vice President, and that they found jarring, and at times even hypocritical, is the fact that he is by roots a populist. He is what I used to call a techno-populist. In other words, he can sit down and talk to you for four hours about the human genome, but the end of it will be, "and we've got to make sure these insurance companies don't screw people with this information." It is, to a large degree, who he is viscerally. As a media person, one of the things you're looking for in a performance is something that's real. Two spots were literally unscripted, him talking. They weren't the first time he'd said it. He'd said it a hundred times. But he kept saying it not only because we told him to, but because he liked it. He felt it was true to him. That's how we got to the fighting language.

SHRUM. That language actually worked. People liked him in that posture.

ESKEW. We drew straws and I lost, so I get to do the "what went wrong." One thing we did wrong was that our campaign ended up in a recount state where our opponent's campaign manager was the chief election official and our opponent's brother was the governor.

SHRUM. And we also did not imagine that we would end up in front of a Supreme Court the vast majority of whose justices were appointed by Republican presidents and at least one of whom had thrown her glass down on the table on election night and said "dammit" when she thought Gore was going to win. Now let's talk about what really went wrong.

ESKEW. We really turned a big ship around and got it going. We got it squarely pointed at Senator Bradley, but we didn't have a contingency plan for success. We stripped the campaign down. We took everybody who was sitting around measuring their drapes for the Oval Office and said, "We've got to go to New Hampshire now, folks," and we doubled up people in rooms and cut the budget. We ran a lean, mean campaign in those states. But we still had this fear of Bradley coming out of New Hampshire.

The fact of the matter is, we came out of Iowa with probably an 8- to 10-point lead in New Hampshire. We only won by four points. The exit polls had us losing. The whole psychology in the press was, "You guys didn't do very well in New Hampshire." That, by the way, disappeared because McCain was the story coming out of New Hampshire.

But we didn't spend February and March as we should have, saying, "Okay, we've won this nomination; we've got to go mop up some states, but this organization is now strategically and po-litically about defeating Governor Bush." We didn't do that. Our campaign was very thin.

That was a big mistake. It let Bush, who had a nightmarish few weeks in which he had to take his game plan—which had been intelligently constructed, probably two years before—and shelve it, and do what he had to do to win. He was able, in this period of March and April and May, to repair damage left over from the primaries, rebuild significantly, and reposition himself as a compassionate conservative. Many of the things he was putting out to the press were interesting and new and different, and we were sitting around fumbling. One week we'd talk about prosperity and progress, and even people in our campaign couldn't remember if it was "progress and prosperity" or "prosperity and progress." We were flat.

SHRUM. Our mistake was that we didn't go seamlessly from the primaries to the general, let the message develop along the lines that fit Al Gore and who he was. Frankly, we spent a couple of months during which Bush was able to rebuild, with at least the sense of invincibility, that he was going to win. Then he went to a convention where, in my view, the convention was all reassurance and no bounce. But that was a victory for Bush, because it allowed him to hold his lead. We couldn't come back into competition in a serious way until our convention. The Pew study showed that 80 percent of the news coverage of Gore was negative up until our convention. We came out of the convention in pretty good shape. Then we came to the debates.

ESKEW. I want to say one thing about this notion of invincibility. I got all the Bush campaign press releases. I didn't get them from a mole; they were sent to me. I didn't read them, because they were endless. But I'd read the headlines, and I'm pretty sure that in the months of March, April, and May at least a third, if not more of them, were about polls. They weren't just polls, they would be "Gore underperforming Clinton in Michigan," "Gore leads in Wisconsin eight points less than what Clinton did." I would look at these things and think, what is this? I figured out that this was a major part of the Bush strategy. It clearly was, up until the very end of the race. I think it was effective. I think it had an impact on the press and the coverage of the campaign. There's no question about it.

Bob Shrum and Carter Eskew. Photo by Kyle Cassidy.

SHRUM. It didn't move voters, in my view, but it moved the press and elites. The Friday before the election, I looked at Stan's numbers and said "This is going to be a very close election; I think the undecideds look like they're going to break to us and we're going to win." I had major national correspondents in effect pat me on the head over the telephone and say, "Bob, it's really sad, you're just crazy. You don't know what you're talking about."

ESKEW. I remember a conversation I had with the Vice President. It was February or March, and he said, "Maybe we ought to have a little Skunk Works project on the expectations game for the debates." Then he looked at me and laughed and said, "Nah, I guess it really wouldn't work." So we had the sense that there was no way that we were going to be able to say that Al Gore wasn't that good a debater, but what we might be able to do was to say George Bush wasn't a bad debater. Ask Ann Richards. Ann's a friend of mine, and she would talk to any reporter who mattered. She said, "Let me tell you about my experience with the guy. I came in there; I thought I killed him, and guess what? The voters thought he did really well." So there were things we tried. But we clearly lost the expectations game, and I'm not sure that we could have won it. The bar was set very low for Bush. Let's face it. He jumped over it, and he deserves credit for that. In the first debate, I remember thinking that Gore won. We had research that immediately followed the debate that suggested he hadn't won. Although it was not a disaster, it was not in any way a clear victory. I felt that it was, in the room. I think what happened was that the Bush team did a really good job, fair and square, of capitalizing and jumping on the so-called misstatements the Vice President made in the debate. Our senior team went off to Kentucky brain dead, having not had any sleep, and said to our press operation, "Well, you take care of this one, this is just a one-day thing. It'll be fixed." It wasn't. It became a very difficult thing for us to deal with, and became the public's perception of the first debate.

SHRUM. Before Stan and Carter and I left for Kentucky, I went into the spin room. I was feeling terrific. There were things I would've changed in the debate, but on the whole I was feeling terrific. It was clear to me right away that the Bush campaign was doing a very good job of changing the standard of judgment about the debate. The standard of judgment was suddenly: "Did Gore make misstatements?" When we were putting this presentation together, I actually had to call around to some of our research and press people, to remember what the so-called misstatements were. One was that he went to a natural disaster with the deputy director of FEMA instead of the director of FEMA. Another was that a Sarasota kid was standing up in her classroom in school, when the truth was that she had been standing up for a long time, but she'd finally gotten a seat. The Bush campaign and the press liked the story because it was interesting. They made this into a very big part of the judgment of the debate. At the same time, Bush was not held accountable for his own misstatements. When asked how much money he spent on health care in Texas, he included all the private charity as though it were part of the state money. That's hardly ever discussed. The second debate was a nonevent except for one critical thing: it allowed Bush to jump the hurdle on foreign policy. He basically bear-hugged Clinton and Gore on foreign policy. At the time, we thought it was a ploy. But I guess he meant it, since he just submitted the Clinton defense budget to Congress.

ESKEW. In the third debate Bush raised serious doubts about himself. When he was asked whether the tax cut does go to the top 1 percent, he said, "Of course it does." He said, "Health insurance. That's a Washington term. What does that mean to people?" Right after that debate, we came to a sense that voters were beginning to worry that Bush wasn't up to the job. The numbers were reaching 48, 49 percent. There was a debate within our campaign whether Gore should say that himself. We decided that he should not. But we did do it in advertising. The Clinton factor was an obsession for the press, and perhaps for some voters. We never completely figured it out. Diane Sawyer did an exclusive interview with Gore. Some of the questions she asked were things like, "You say you grew up on farm. If you grew up on a farm, what side of the fence are the boards on? Did they face your farm? Are they outside the posts?" to trap him. But a lot of the questions had to do with Clinton. "Do you still think he's the greatest President in history?" It was all about 17 degrees of separation from Clinton. It sort of overwhelmed the announcement.

What's interesting about that is that recently in Washington there was a story on the front page of the *Washington Post* about a meeting the Vice President and the President had after the election. No one was there except the President and Vice President, but this is often the case. There was reporting on it, nonetheless, and it was described variously as a very explosive meeting and as a very cathartic meeting. Nonetheless, it dominated the political news cycle for 24–48 hours, to the point where the *Today Show* called me and said, "We'll send a satellite truck for you at 6:00 A.M. We want you to be the top of the segment." So it just doesn't go away. I mean here we are, sixty days after the election, and they're still fascinated by it. We had a hard time figuring this thing out. The first question of the first debate in New Hampshire was about Bill Clinton.

SHRUM. There was a period of time when it worked. The hand-off in Macomb County during the Democratic convention and the first night of the convention were examples. The press did not understand that Clinton's speech actually helped move the numbers in the right direction. The second night of the convention, people thought "Why are these liberals speaking?" The truth was, we began to open up a very big advantage on health care. The Gore speech in which he asked people to see him as his own man and judge him for who he really was, the postconvention period, it all worked.

In the last week, it came back again. Clinton became a big question. Frankly, we made hard decisions based on the data whether to use him or not. A lot of the climate of scandal surrounding him was unfair, but it was something that we had to deal with. And we dealt with it. The President gave us extraordinary political and financial support, but for a lot of the swing voters, the election was as much or more about restoring honor and integrity to the White House as it was about the economy. That's why Bush kept saying it. The bottom line on our shortcomings? We didn't convince enough voters that Al Gore was his own man not only to carry the popular vote and carry Florida relatively narrowly but to provide a cushion against the Florida factor and the Supreme Court ploy.

LIONEL SOSA (Bush campaign). This meeting where the two men finally got out how they were feeling personally about each other—I can't help but think that had to affect everything, if these feelings between the two top men have never been addressed, wouldn't this, from a managerial point of view, affect the whole campaign? Rather than say, "This is how we're going to win," having the thought that Clinton will come in and suck up the air if he lets him, or wavering over whether Clinton should be there at all. How much did that affect the campaign? Was that a big factor, or a nonfactor?

SHRUM. I think it affected the campaign externally far more than it did internally. A number of us—Bill Daley, Carter, myself—at various times talked to the President directly about the campaign. He was very useful. He had very good advice. He was very practical about where he should go and where he could help and where he could not help. Frankly, in the last week a lot of the pressure on where he should go was not coming from him; it was coming from other office holders. One friend of mine, in a Midwestern state which we ultimately carried, said, "We have to have Clinton. We have to have Clinton. We have to have Clinton" during a discussion with me on the phone. I finally said, "Look, I don't think the President particularly wants to come. He knows what the numbers are there." The President was very practical about this. As an operational issue internally, it was not difficult. As an external issue, and a fascination with the press, it was constantly difficult. Internally, the senior White House staff were incredibly cooperative and helpful. So was the President. He worked really hard, raised a ton of money for us, and was very open in strategic discussions. He offered good advice. That was not the problem. There was no tension between the camps sucking energy or time out of our campaign. It was the constant interest on the part of the press about their relationship that was the problem.

KATHLEEN HALL JAMIESON (University of Pennsylvania). You suggested that your data showed, after the first debate, that Gore might not have done as well as you thought. Our data suggest that among those who watched the debate the perception was that he had won, and for the week following they continued in that perception. So if you watched the debate, you continued to perceive that he won. But those who didn't watch the debate increasingly perceived that he had not won. That would suggest to us that that was a media effect not a debate effect, and we're wondering if you could sort that out for us.

SHRUM. Our data were coming from undecided voters, not from a general population. They were coming from focus groups. I think Gore won the first debate. In other words, we thought we did well in the first debate, even though some of our data suggest that with undecided voters we didn't do as well as we thought. But clearly, the effect of the Bush campaign's skillful exploitation of some of the mistakes did drive the press coverage of the debate, which then influenced many millions of others who had not seen the debate.

RUTH MANDEL (Rutgers University). The work that I have seen on the presidential–vice presidential hand-offs suggests that there's a conflict between the president's concern for his legacy and his willingness to tout whatever a vice president has done. If you look at what Clinton did in the period of this campaign, you'll see him trying to be fair to Al Gore and then slipping back into the kind of discourse that's more concerned with his own legacy. That may be the tension more than other things.

SHRUM. The electorate had what I call cognitive dissonance about Clinton. They thought he had been a terrific president, but had doubts about personal approval of him. But I think your comment's very interesting. Eisenhower gave Nixon the complete cold shoulder. He destroyed him in one press conference answer when a reporter said, "The Vice President's running on all the important things he's done during your administration. Can you name something?" And he said, "Give me five minutes and I might think of something," which became, by the way, one of the first negative ads by the Kennedy campaign in 1960.

Ronald Reagan would not endorse George Bush during the Republican primaries in 1988. I do not believe that the so-called problem between Bill Clinton and Al Gore was a problem between Bill Clinton and Al Gore. It was an obsession with the press. It was a great story. Therefore, they had to write this story, and it was all tied up in the aftermath of impeachment and whether the press felt the President had gotten what he deserved or not, and how that was going to play with Gore.

But the natural human tendency of the President, in terms of claiming a legacy, is occasionally to say, "And by the way, I did that, too." I don't think that was a problem for us. In fact, I think some day somebody's gonna stand back from this and say, "In a hundred years, there were three other Vice Presidents who ran directly to succeed presidents. Nixon lost to Kennedy, Humphrey lost to Nixon, and Bush beat Dukakis. Gore won *and* lost." I think it's always going to be complicated for a vice president. It's a great advantage in running for the nomination, but it has real complications in the general election.

JAMIESON. Could you speak to the Republican analysis that you were hurt by Gore on Elian Gonzalez and the release of oil from the strategic petroleum reserves?

ESKEW. Elian Gonzalez did hurt us. We managed to take a principled decision and make it look both unprincipled and stupid, which is hard to do.

That period of what I call the Big Sleep affected our campaign. Al Gore is much more conservative on foreign policy than many Democrats, certainly more than many Americans assume. He doesn't like the Castro regime. He did not necessarily trust the normal channels for dealing with immigration in a case where a boy has come to this country and his mother has died in the process. He thought it should go to family court. I think he felt that there should be some time to see whether people were speaking freely. He took that position in Iowa in the "Black-Brown Debate" in January. It was at that point not a big story. He reiterated it in New Hampshire, and I think he may have reiterated it in the Harlem debate, where it was more of an issue. There was the sense that people were saying he was treating this kid differently than he might treat a Haitian. But when it really surfaced was when the Clinton administration made a move not to put it in family court, or to leave it with INS. I don't remember exactly.

We had to speak out, to break with the administration, and to keep the same position we had.

At that point, it became a big huge deal. It looked as if all it was about was pandering to Cuban-Americans in Miami, that Gore was willing to break with his own administration. Nobody liked the decision. The Black Caucus hated the decision. Very few people liked the decision, and that is a case where the campaign failed the candidate. We didn't foresee this. We should have done a lot more briefing of columnists, and we should have had the Vice President make a speech and say, "Look, I understand this is controversial, but here's why I'm doing it." It played into the sense of political opportunism. One of Bush's lines was, "He'll say or do anything to be president."

The petroleum reserve issue was a little different, but I can see how it could have been perceived that way. I don't have any data on that. That was done in the context of an overall energy policy, but looked completely divorced from it, and looked also as if he was willing to use a national strategic resource for political purposes. Interestingly enough, the spot market prices fell after the petroleum release. It might actually have been good public policy. But it was difficult to convince people of that with three weeks to go in an election.

SHRUM. By the way, on Elian, I think we would have had trouble, because the elites generally are anti-anti-Castro. The petroleum reserve was a right decision on policy that hurt us in the short term. But in the long term was probably either neutral or slightly beneficial, but it wasn't made for that reason.

Three

Stanley Greenberg

Stanley Greenberg is Chairman and Chief Executive Officer of Greenberg Research, a strategic research firm for campaigns, private-sector organizations, and public interest groups. Mr. Greenberg has advised a broad range of campaigns including those of President Bill Clinton and Vice President Al Gore, Senators Joe Lieberman and Chris Dodd, as well as a number of candidates for the U.S. Congress. For many years he served as principal polling adviser to the Democratic National Committee. He has also conducted extensive research overseas, serving as polling adviser to the national campaigns of politicians such as Nelson Mandela and Tony Blair. Mr. Greenberg received his Ph.D. from Harvard University and spent a decade teaching at Yale, where he received a Guggenheim Fellowship before establishing Greenberg Research in 1980.

Many of us who view the world through polling try to begin with a respect for the public consciousness and the understanding the public brings to electoral decisions. The political communication becomes a kind of contract, or bond, that does have a powerful impact on what people do in government. This is frequently diminished by what happens in campaigns, and it's frequently diminished by the media. I don't think this was one of the elections where that was true. I think the media did a better job, and a more elevated job, than the campaigns did. I should also thank Bob Shrum and Carter Eskew and Tad Devine and others who are not here, because they graciously brought me into the campaign in July. Timing's everything. I did not have to bear up through the primaries and that long process. I had a fresh look at this, and they expressed confidence and gave me the authority to deal with polling and strategy issues in that period. I should also mention that this was a very comfortable campaign internally. On some of the issues that were discussed here, whether they have to do with overall thematic position or target states, or how to deal with the President, there was a strategic unity within the campaign and it was, day to day, a fairly harmonious campaign. I don't do this for spin. I'm happy to talk about it afterward, because there's a temptation to report on whatever little divide one can find. That was not the dominant mood of this campaign. This was a campaign that woke up most days ready to fight, feeling confident of where they were going.

I should mention that I come here from Israel. When you think about good and bad moments in campaigns, reflect on the fact that in the last week people were dying each day in drive-by shootings and other terrorist acts. Reflect on the failure of our signature agenda item, the peace process. The negotiations are at a standstill, and Arafat has a favorability rating of 6 percent. The general strike is going on, with our support of labor unions. The garbage is piling up and the economy is going into a recession in the last quarter. With our phantom opponent within the party challenging us up until the Friday before the election, you should think about the tameness of the campaigns that we just went through and the set of forces that worked for us and against us on both sides.

The campaign mattered. The campaigns run and the themes used clearly affected the outcome. I'll begin with the election we

Stanley Greenberg. Photo by Kyle Cassidy.

won, in which we got the largest popular vote, and the center-left got a larger 52 percent of the vote.

I mention that not so much for whether I get to put Gore 2000 on the win or loss side of the Web site, but because it's very important to the debates, particularly on the Democratic side, on where we go from here.

It's very important to learn the right lessons from the election. The lesson not to learn is that the Democrats lost this election. I will argue here that when you look at thematic positioning, or issue positioning, or the economy, or at mobilization of base, that the Gore campaign was dominant on all of those elements and should have been in a position to build an even stronger majority than that they achieved.

The burden becomes to explain whether that's all true. You're dominant on theme and issues and economy, and you mobilized your voters. Why was there not a bigger majority for Al Gore, so we didn't have to have this bickering over a few hundred votes in Florida? There isn't one single positioning or strategy that could have put George Bush in the White House, and there was not only one strategy for getting to the majority that we had. But we did have a strategy for a Democratic majority, and we executed it and achieved it.

This was a survey done for the Campaign for America's Future and for Democracy Corps. It was released right after the election. It was done on election night and the day after. It asked people basic, overall thematic positioning of the two campaigns. This was something close to what we had used or developed over time:

> Al Gore says America put its house in order and has the opportunity to make sure all are enriched by our prosperity, but George Bush squanders the surplus on a massive tax cut for the wealthiest few. His plans would draw a trillion dollars out of Social Security. Gore says we should make a choice that reflects our values. We should balance the budget, pay down the national debt, continue our prosperity. We must cut middle class taxes and defend education, Medicare, and Social Security. We should make our prosperity work for all.

This is not a caricature of our message. It was our message, though it does reflect the evolution of our message over the course of the public campaign. Campaigns do not fix a message in concrete and though our message evolved as we expected it would, that was the core message we tested against it. Missing from the Bush message is the value side. It's purposely not in here, because the key here was to see whether the overall position on spending, budget surplus, role of government weakened the Gore position in this election.

George Bush says the people created our surplus and prosperity, not the government. Al Gore thinks it's the government's money. He favors big government solutions to every problem. I trust the people, he trusts the government. Some of the surplus should be returned to the people through a tax cut. We should do more to renew education and help seniors with prescription drugs. I want more local control and accountability in schools. Bush says, "I trust the people to invest their Social Security and make choices in health care."

We won that choice by 17 points on Election Day this year. Fifty-four percent voted for the Gore message, essentially on the broad role of government and the view that they wanted to extend and continue the prosperity with a strong economic performance as well as make sure that the economy works for all.

It was a populist formulation. There is a temptation in talking about the populist formulation to turn it into attacks on insurance companies and HMOs or prescription drug companies. That was an element of it. It was just an element. If you look at Al Gore's convention speech, the words he used are fairly moderate. He says sometimes you need to have a leader who is willing to say no to the prescription drug companies or the HMOs, so that the people will benefit.

It was an important part of the overall message. It reinforced

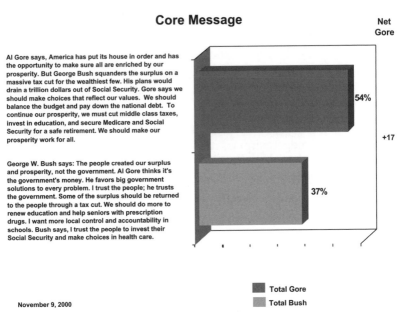

Core Message

Net Gore

Al Gore says, America has put its house in order and has the opportunity to make sure all are enriched by our prosperity. But George Bush squanders the surplus on a massive tax cut for the wealthiest few. His plans would drain a trillion dollars out of Social Security. Gore says we should make choices that reflect our values. We should balance the budget and pay down the national debt. To continue our prosperity, we must cut middle class taxes, invest in education, and secure Medicare and Social Security for a safe retirement. We should make our prosperity work for all.

George W. Bush says: The people created our surplus and prosperity, not the government. Al Gore thinks it's the government's money. He favors big government solutions to every problem. I trust the people; he trusts the government. Some of the surplus should be returned to the people through a tax cut. We should do more to renew education and help seniors with prescription drugs. I want more local control and accountability in schools. Bush says, I trust the people to invest their Social Security and make choices in health care.

54%

+17

37%

November 9, 2000

■ Total Gore
■ Total Bush

the authenticity of Al Gore because he was willing to take on big interests. But the overall thematic position was to make sure our prosperity enriches all. Our populist formulation was not one that walked away from the economy. It presumed a strong economy, wanted to extend it into the future.

The next graph is from the campaign's early research.

The formulation of the Bush contrast is not very strong at this point. Later, we used Bush's actual language. But we tried this contrast: "With the current prosperity and surplus, this is the time to make sure that our prosperity enriches not just a few, but all hard-working families. We should invest in education, middle-class tax cuts, and a secure retirement."

We counterposed that to a Bush statement: "With the current prosperity, it's the time to lock up Social Security, return the bulk of the surplus to the people, cut taxes across the board, return the money to the people."

Populist Element

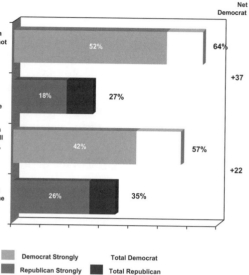

Net
Democrat

With the current prosperity and surplus, this is a time to make sure that our prosperity enriches not just the few but all working families. We should invest in education, middle class tax cuts and a secure retirement
— 52%   64%

With the current prosperity and surplus, this is the time to lock up Social Security and then return the bulk of the surplus to the people. We should cut taxes across the board and return the money to the people
— 18%   27%   +37

With the current prosperity and surplus, this is a time to make sure that our prosperity enriches all working families. We should invest in education, middle class tax cuts and a secure retirement.
— 42%   57%

With the current prosperity and surplus, this is the time to lock up Social Security and then return the bulk of the surplus to the people. We should cut taxes across the board and return the money to the people
— 26%   35%   +22

Democrat Strongly   Total Democrat
Republican Strongly   Total Republican

August 24, 2000

Core Message: Prosperity At Risk

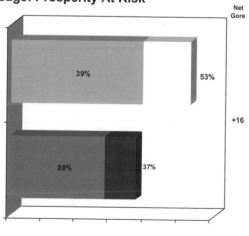

Net
Gore

Gore Says, America's prosperity is at stake in this election. George Bush puts that prosperity at risk. He squanders our surplus on a massive tax cut for the wealthiest 1 percent and drains a trillion dollars from Social Security. 300 economists say his plans will increase the national debt, raise interest rates and threaten economic growth. Gore says, we should balance the budget and pay down the national debt. To continue our prosperity, we must cut middle class taxes, invest in education and secure retirement.
— 39%   53%

Bush says, Gore favors national, one-size-fits-all solutions to every problem. But I trust the people to make choices, not Washington politicians. Some of the federal surplus should be returned to the people through a tax cut. We should do more to renew education and help seniors with prescription drugs. But I want more local control and accountability in schools. Bush says, I trust people to invest their Social Security and make choices in health care.
— 28%   37%   +16

Gore Strongly   Total Gore
Bush Strongly   Total Bush

October 15, 2000

We won that contrast by 37 points.

Keep in mind, this was a test done by the campaign in July. The two lower bars in the first chart immediately above are the exact same test without the formulation that says "for the many, not the few." The message that had "the many, not the few" part of it was about 15 points stronger.

So we wanted to talk about extending the prosperity, but the populist element to that prosperity was a much more powerful formulation in terms of the voters responding. This was done in July. The backdrop for Al Gore's candidacy in this election was not the '96 election. It was the period prior to this, with impeachment and protracted battle around the President, which had produced a midterm election in '98 in which Democrats gained with turnout among low-income minority voters and union voters and gained at the top level, with the better educated voters, reacting against the assault on privacy and the cultural preoccupations of the conservatives.

But Democrats lost in the '98 elections with white, non-college-educated men and women, particularly women. The non-college-educated white women, whom Bill Clinton had done pretty well with, pulled away during the impeachment battle. This group was very much in our sights at the convention. That's who we were trying to reach, and in fact, that's who we moved. Some people say our message was aimed at base voters. It was not aimed at base voters. It was aimed at the swing voters. It was constantly who we were trying to reach. They were in western Pennsylvania, they were in blue-collar and lower middle-income suburbs of cities around the country, and those voters moved very strongly after the convention.

The overall thematic position I described was very much at the center of what the campaign was doing in the period after the convention. There are a number of things that happened. At the convention, Al Gore and his family commitments were introduced via a biography. People really focused on him as a potentially strong leader for the first time. The campaign ran the sixty-second "Biography" ad through the month of August into September. This is the polling from the campaign for the four-way presidential vote and is followed by the two-way vote. The beginning of the chart is when I joined the campaign. I should mention in terms of this issue of polling, we poll nationally as well as state. Harrison Hickman did all the state polling. The national polling worked with models made by Sam Popkin using elections back to 1992. This election, about three-quarters of the

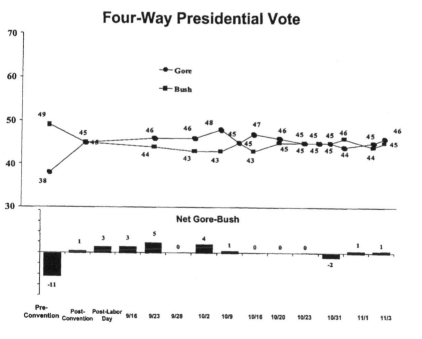

Four-Way Presidential Vote

Net Gore-Bush

variance in the rank-order of the states is explained by what's happening in the national number.

There are things happening state by state, but the country as a whole is moving one way or the other. Most of our strategic thematic work took place within national polls, and we would test it out within the states. It led us to a more unitary kind of message out of our overall polling. I put this up to highlight the period from what happened in the convention, when the race went even, then we began to pull ahead to Labor Day and then almost to the end of July. I highlight this because it is a period where there was a thematic battle. We laid out this message as clear as could be in our advertising. We were attacked on big government, and all those attacks came in that period. I'll show you the two-way votes dropping Nader and Buchanan out, because it illustrates how wide the lead was during this period of thematic battle.

For us, that was important because this is not an academic exercise. We wanted to move the Nader voters to us at the end of the election. I actually think that's why, in part, the late deciders broke for us. Nader's voters were a significant part of the late deciders or switchers. But we built up a substantial lead in the two-way contest going to the end of July. It changed. I'll highlight the change here and come back later to the question of why we didn't have a larger majority. It changed on two things.

One, there was one week in which we faced not just the strategic petroleum reserve, but the prescription drug misstatement on the cost of his mother's and his pet's prescription drugs, which introduced this question of exaggeration, which then went into the strategic petroleum reserve, which together said, he'll say anything political, exaggerate, and that reinforced the trust problems.

We dropped in our own polls. We dropped 4 points that week, so it did have an impact. It came right back. It was not something that changed the structure of the race. It came back to the week before the debate. We went into the debate with a 4-point lead in our polls, which disappeared with the first debate. So there was an immediate and strong impact from the debate. It's important to understand that we believed thematically, both during the period of time in which there was thematic debate, and after the election, that this is not a situation where there is nothing to explain. The overall thematic positioning was just fine. The alternative model for running would have been to run on continuity. Believe me, one of the frustrations of the campaign was why we couldn't run on the economy. Every message we tested that tried to run on the

Two-Way Presidential Vote

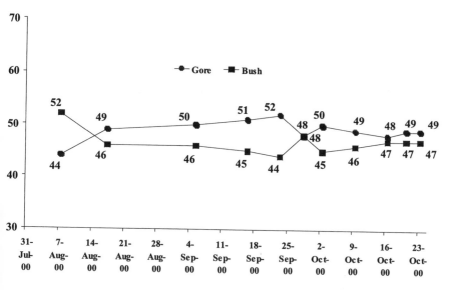

past economy didn't work. I saw Mark Penn's research in that period, which also focused on the economy and did not get very far. There were a number of reasons why the economy did not work as a message at that point.

It goes back to Fred Steeper's point. Before the Democratic convention, Al Gore was seen as a weak leader. Not because he is intrinsically a weak leader but because vice presidents are seen as weak leaders, and in this case, in the shadow of a very strong president—or at least a very big presence—Al Gore was seen to be weak. The issues of trust were there going into this convention. Anything that we tried taking credit for the economy at that point, we found just did not work. It was not believable. In fact, it reinforced the sense that he was exaggerating and taking credit for things that were not real. Plus Bush's perception of having a distinguished political family and being a strong leader comes independently of anything that George Bush did. Al Gore was not known to be from a political family. It was one of the things that was introduced at the convention. Being part of a political family says you've come to politics through things other than ambition, that it's part of family values and there's a leadership quality that's part of that family. George Bush had that coming in. He was seen as strong, and I believe that affected the perception of his ability to handle the economy. Plus, he was a pro-business, pro-market Republican. He seemed reasonable, not crazy. At that point, we were reasonably competitive on the question of the economy. This is not something figured out after the fact.

The plan at the time was to base our message on the economy, presume the prosperity, make sure it works for all, and in the last month of the campaign, after we have emerged on the stage, appear to have leadership strength and after we have built up doubts about George Bush, not just on the economy, but on risky proposals and on a bad record in Texas, after that was established, then deliver the message warning of endangering the economy with George Bush. If you look at our advertising in the last four weeks of the campaign, all the positive advertising begins with our prosperity. Extend it, don't put it at risk. That was absolutely central to the plan of the campaign, which we executed. At the end of the day, in the research that we have here, in the postelection research, we started with about a three-point advantage on the economy.

We ended the election with a 9-point advantage on the economy. In Mark Penn's postelection research, Al Gore was 14 points ahead of George Bush on who would better extend the prosperity. We had an alternative strategy on the economy, and that was to run on the strategy, but to zigzag our way there, not to try to hammer through by taking control of it at the outset. In the end, I believe that we did. The campaign never stopped. It never let up.

From August right through to Election Day, there was a negative track that always talked about George Bush's failed record in Texas. The poll data continued to rise, particularly after the third debate, in the sense of whether he was up to the up to the job.

We linked "Not up to the job," "Bad record in Texas," "Crazy proposals on Social Security," and "A tax cut for the top one percent." "Don't trust him with our prosperity" was the heart of the closing argument for the campaign.

This research comes out of Harrison Hickman's research, which is the Clinton favorability. Very favorable and very unfavorable responses to Bill Clinton in each of the battleground states. This was done in early October. We had a situation dealing with the President. I worked for Bill Clinton. I think Bill Clinton did an exceptional job as president. I would have recommended anything in this campaign that would help us win this race. The question of Bill Clinton's role was not actually a serious question. It was not a serious debate within the campaign. It came later, from outside, but it was not a serious debate in the campaign. There are two aspects to Bill Clinton. There is his job approval and there is his personal favorability. I've run an analysis to predict the vote with only two pieces of data—job approval rating for Bill Clinton and personal favorability of Bill Clinton.

First of all, the two variables predict 62 percent of the variance in the vote. Bill Clinton was significant to what people were doing in this election. The other interesting thing is that job approval and personal favorability are exactly equal in their impact on affecting the vote. One has a coefficient of .41, one of .42. People's personal feelings about Bill Clinton and their assessment approval were equally important. Clearly, some models use job approval as their only factor.

Now this may be specific to Bill Clinton. It may be specific to an era in which personal character has become much more of a public issue. It may be a function of an eight-year cultural war waged by the right to bring down Bill Clinton, which I think has helped make the personal character a part of the voting decision. There are a lot of reasons for it, but the fact is, personality and

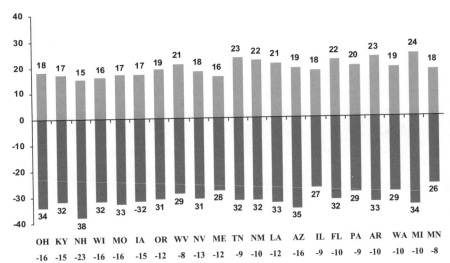

The Clinton Factor

performance were equally important in how people were voting in this election.

If you look at the graph, this was not a hard decision. New Hampshire net -23 on the personal unfavorability versus favorability. Ohio, -16, Wisconsin, -16, Missouri, -16, Arizona, -16, Kentucky, all the states with fairly large rural and small town populations that were in the battleground. These were short discussions internally.

It was obvious. If we were running a popular election without the Electoral College and it was simply a question of building up a national majority, I'm not sure what conclusion I'd draw on what to do in this election. But it was very clear that if our goal was to win an Electoral College majority, this was not the way to do it.

We asked the question periodically whether, after eight years of the Clinton/Gore administration, it was time for a change, or

The Clinton Factor

Bill Clinton 's Favorability	Strongly Favorable	Strongly Unfavorable	Difference	Total Favorable	Total Unfavorable	Total Difference
Minnesota	18	26	-8	44	42	2
Michigan	24	34	-10	44	45	1
Washington	19	29	-10	44	43	1
Arkansas	23	33	-10	46	46	0
Pennsylvania	20	29	-9	42	42	0
Florida	22	32	-10	44	45	-1
Illinois	18	27	-9	42	43	-1
Arizona	19	35	-16	43	47	-4
Louisiana	21	33	-12	43	47	-4
New Mexico	22	32	-10	42	46	-4
Tennessee	23	32	-9	43	48	-5
Maine	16	28	-12	40	46	-6
Nevada	18	31	-13	41	47	-6
West Virginia	21	29	-8	40	46	-6
Oregon	19	31	-12	40	47	-7
Iowa	17	32	-15	39	46	-7
Missouri	17	33	-16	40	48	-8
Wisconsin	16	32	-16	39	47	-8
New Hampshire	15	38	-23	38	47	-9
Kentucky	17	32	-15	39	50	-11
Ohio	18	34	-16	38	50	-12

Continue or Change

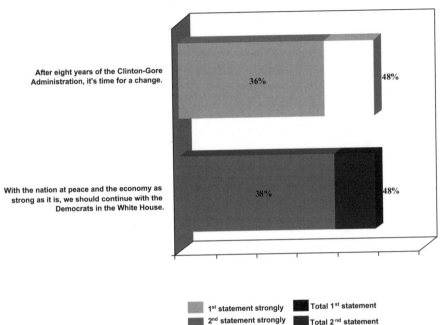

After eight years of the Clinton-Gore Administration, it's time for a change.   36%   48%

With the nation at peace and the economy as strong as it is, we should continue with the Democrats in the White House.   38%   48%

1st statement strongly   Total 1st statement
2nd statement strongly   Total 2nd statement

whether, with the nation at peace and the economy strong, we should continue with the Democrats in the White House.

The result was 48/48. This was even though people thought the country was moving in the right direction. People were concerned with lots of things: the moral decline in the country, social decay. When you got to the question of, do I want to continue or do I want change, the country was divided 48/48. They were divided pretty much 48/48 on how they voted.

Deciding how to approach this strategically—what theme, what choice—was not done out of personal pique. If Gore and Clinton had only met earlier, we might have come together. If their embracing was the best way forward, I'm for it. People had

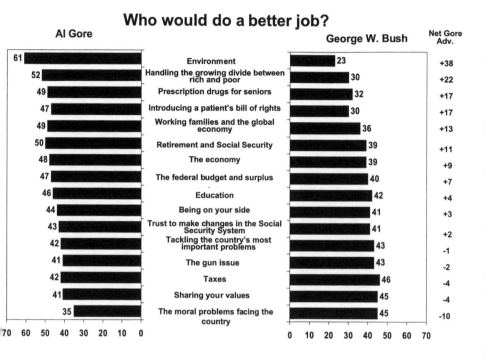

Who would do a better job?

Al Gore		George W. Bush	Net Gore Adv.
61	Environment	23	+38
52	Handling the growing divide between rich and poor	30	+22
49	Prescription drugs for seniors	32	+17
47	Introducing a patient's bill of rights	30	+17
49	Working families and the global economy	36	+13
50	Retirement and Social Security	39	+11
48	The economy	39	+9
47	The federal budget and surplus	40	+7
46	Education	42	+4
44	Being on your side	41	+3
43	Trust to make changes in the Social Security System	41	+2
42	Tackling the country's most important problems	43	-1
41	The gun issue	43	-2
42	Taxes	46	-4
41	Sharing your values	45	-4
35	The moral problems facing the country	45	-10

complicated views in this election. My focus was on the cultural war. This war started in '92 in New Hampshire. It was fought in '94 with Gingrich, and then the right was robbed of victory in '96 when Bill Clinton was reelected. They thought they could get him impeached and they failed. This election was the last chapter in that battle.

Al Gore and the Democrats were very much taken up in that war. It affected perceptions, and it affected the strategic choices that we could make. This is a list of a range of issues.

This was a poll done election night, right after the election, on which party is better on the various issues. It's a kind of report card on what happened in this election. On questions of social in-

surance, like HMO reform, prescription drugs, we won those issues in the end, though we had to battle them. We paid a high
price for that, but not on the issue itself. We beat George Bush on
prescription drugs and on Social Security, but Bush looked like
he wanted to do something. He didn't look like a man with bad
intentions. It also put us on seniors' issues for a much longer period than we wanted to be. One of the reasons we did not get to
youth-oriented and education issues—which we did somewhat,
but not to anywhere near the degree that we wanted to—was that
we could not walk away from the battles we were fighting on prescription drugs and Social Security.

We knew that there was some interest in the issue of privatization. There was no formulation around the privatization that we
saw as having a great electoral advantage. What we had was a
candidate who was consumed with the fact that George Bush had
made a trillion-dollar promise that did not appear anywhere in his
budget, and that he was going to leave somebody else to figure
out how to pay. The candidate was consumed with that. He was
insistent that it was wrong that George Bush be able to get away
with that. We spent a lot of time trying to figure out how to go
with the issue.

Eventually we settled on a way of going at it that addressed
people's cynicism about very big promises. He was promising the
same trillion dollars to young workers and to seniors at the same
time. Which promise was he going to break? We went after Social Security not on roulette. We didn't run anything on the
roulette, as a gamble using the stock market. We ran after it on a
number of levels. One, that he was making promises he couldn't
keep. Pulling a trillion dollars out of Social Security is going to
endanger Social Security. Then we linked it to the economy. Our
overall message was that if he drained a trillion dollars out of Social Security, it would endanger the economy. We tried to convey
the sense that he was risky. But it was not on the investment in the

stock market, it was on budget calculation.

It was a very powerful attack, one of our highest-testing ads. It was never answered. George Bush couldn't answer it. It was one of the reasons why we won on the economy.

We won the prescription drugs by 17 points, patient's bill of rights by 17 points, retirement, Social Security by 11. We won the economy in this poll by 9 at the end. We started in the low single digits and we moved on the economy. In the last two weeks, the message that we were using on the economy was working. We moved up on the economy and were 10 points ahead in our own internal polls.

The postelection had 9, and Penn's poll has 14. But we won on the economy, and that lead grew over the last couple of weeks. On who you trust to handle the federal budget and surplus, we had 7 points.

Now, for a Democrat to finish with a 7-point advantage on handling the federal budget and surplus. I'm not sure I trust Democrats to have that much money in their hands. But by 7 points, the voters trusted Al Gore more than George Bush. Penn's postelection survey on which candidate was more fiscally responsible said Al Gore by 3 points. We ran as a fiscal conservative candidate, but we were seen to be responsible. We're going to pay down the national debt.

We were not the big spender in the race. On education, we won by 4, which was clearly unacceptable as a Democrat. Part of the reason that George Bush did a good job on this issue was the battles we fought among seniors.

Tackling the country's most important problems was basically even at the end, and I do think that Bush got credit for a willingness, on education and Social Security, to talk about some big ideas, and was seen to be addressing the country's problems. Taxes: Bush had only a -4 advantage. Now this is a signature issue. For a Democrat to be behind by only 4 points on taxes and for that to be the signature issue of your campaign, says that your message overall has not been effective in the main battleground of ideas between the campaigns.

The two problem areas. First, "shared your values." We were -4 overall on which candidate shared your values. We were -14 among white voters on shared your values. On the moral problems facing the country, we were down 10 points at the end of the campaign. That's clearly where the Bush campaign got its main advantage. The issue advantages that we gained translated into what people said they were doing when they were voting.

We asked people who voted for Al Gore or ever considered voting for Al Gore, in order not to have in consideration hard-line Republicans. Hard-line Bush supporters were never in play. In a postelection survey, we asked those voters why they voted for Al Gore. The number one issue was protecting Social Security and providing prescription drug benefits for seniors. Seniors moved to us at the end. It was an important part of Florida being competitive. Lowering class size and improving education was number two. A woman's right to choose was very important, both as a reason to vote for Al Gore and a reason not to vote for George Bush. Middle class tax cuts for education and the environment were also important.

Balancing the budget and paying down the national debt—who would have thought that we'd have a Democrat elected where among the top reasons given for voting for him is retiring the national debt?

His fiscal prudence was an important part of his overall position. Then there's a collection of things—making our prosperity enrich all families, willingness to stand up to the HMOs, opposition to Bush's massive tax cut. Together, these introduced a populist element. The populist elements were stronger in doubts about Bush. The campaign played on who George Bush was.

This was not a race just about us, this was a choice. The populist positioning enabled us to present George Bush as a problem, as risky, planning to privatize and take a trillion dollars out of Social Security.

This was the single biggest reason people gave for not voting for George Bush. It was not the stock market, it was the budget and that he was playing with a trust fund and promising it to two groups.

His opposition to a woman's right to choose was a top reason to vote against him. His favoring the wealthiest and most privileged, and his inexperience and the Texas record were more reasons why people were against him. Overall, we were raising the kinds of doubts we needed to.

Reasons to Vote for Al Gore

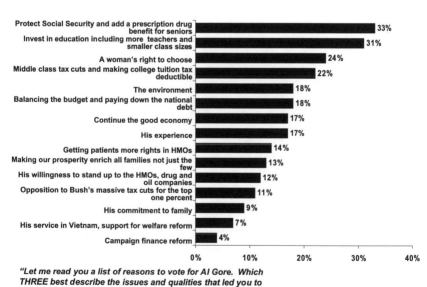

Protect Social Security and add a prescription drug benefit for seniors	33%
Invest in education including more teachers and smaller class sizes	31%
A woman's right to choose	24%
Middle class tax cuts and making college tuition tax deductible	22%
The environment	18%
Balancing the budget and paying down the national debt	18%
Continue the good economy	17%
His experience	17%
Getting patients more rights in HMOs	14%
Making our prosperity enrich all families not just the few	13%
His willingness to stand up to the HMOs, drug and oil companies	12%
Opposition to Bush's massive tax cuts for the top one percent	11%
His commitment to family	9%
His service in Vietnam, support for welfare reform	7%
Campaign finance reform	4%

"Let me read you a list of reasons to vote for Al Gore. Which THREE best describe the issues and qualities that led you to vote for/consider voting for him?"

November 9, 2000

Doubts about Voting for George W. Bush

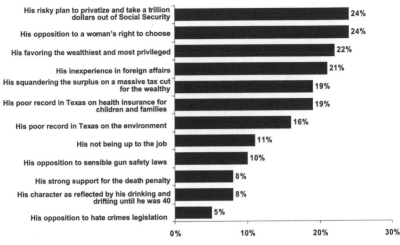

His risky plan to privatize and take a trillion dollars out of Social Security	24%
His opposition to a woman's right to choose	24%
His favoring the wealthiest and most privileged	22%
His inexperience in foreign affairs	21%
His squandering the surplus on a massive tax cut for the wealthy	19%
His poor record in Texas on health insurance for children and families	19%
His poor record in Texas on the environment	16%
His not being up to the job	11%
His opposition to sensible gun safety laws	10%
His strong support for the death penalty	8%
His character as reflected by his drinking and drifting until he was 40	8%
His opposition to hate crimes legislation	5%

"Let me read you a list of doubts about George W. Bush. Regardless of how you voted, which THREE describe the best reasons for not voting for him?"

November 9, 2000

Stanley Greenberg. Photo by Kyle Cassidy.

So if we had a thematically dominant position, if we won on the issues we needed to win on, and minimized Bush's advantage on others, if we raised doubts about him that were central to a choice that favored us, and won on the economy, why does the other guy have the big house? Let me talk about three factors. There's disingenuousness about this. It's easy to talk about the strengths, a little bit harder to talk about the failings. I'm not going to talk about the failings. I'll leave that to others, because Al Gore is a central part of this, and I came out of this with an immense respect for Al Gore. His discomfort in a political space is something I came to admire in him.

He clearly has strong beliefs. He is smart, committed to family, and he fights for things even though they're unpopular. He didn't have the easy facility some other politicians have of moving into a public space with private values and operating comfortably. He wasn't that comfortable in the public space, but I view that as a measure of character.

Let me start with the cultural question. There are some reinforcing things going on. This goes back to the environment in which this election took place, in the context of the cultural war waged against the Clinton administration and against Bill Clinton. But it's also reinforced by some things that have happened in this election. The reasons people gave for voting against Al Gore were heavily concentrated on cultural issues: the positions he took on gay unions, abortion, and guns. There was a Democratic primary some people were paying attention to, in which Democrats competed regarding who might have deviated fourteen years ago on parental notification, who had the strongest position on guns (whether it was the registration of gun owners or issues entirely out of the plausible public debate in the Congress), and on gay unions, which was not an issue the public had moved toward. They were fine on issues of employment discrimination, but on these other questions the public was not there. Those positions were fought in the Democratic primary. What I discovered in debate prep was, these views were not just primary positions. These were views Al Gore felt, believed, and wanted to talk about. He brought to this campaign a commitment on those issues that was real and serious.

But it also played into the cultural doubts people had about Democrats, and suggested that even though the convention had introduced a strong sense of family and values, the specific positions were culturally distancing Al Gore from many of the voters. Many of the reasons those non-college white women and men did not come back was because of those cultural issues. You then get to a second set of issues around trust—exaggerations of truthfulness, being too close to the Clintons. There arises another set of doubts about him. Then you get a third set of doubts, which has to do with different aspects of the role of government—sup-

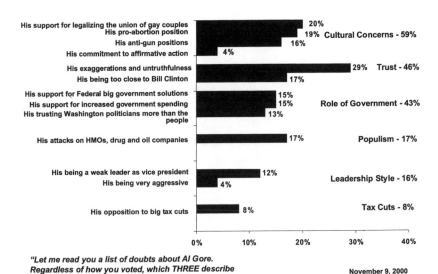

Doubts about Voting for Al Gore

His support for legalizing the union of gay couples — 20%
His pro-abortion position — 19%   Cultural Concerns - 59%
His anti-gun positions — 16%
His commitment to affirmative action — 4%

His exaggerations and untruthfulness — 29%   Trust - 46%
His being too close to Bill Clinton — 17%

His support for Federal big government solutions — 15%
His support for increased government spending — 15%   Role of Government - 43%
His trusting Washington politicians more than the people — 13%

His attacks on HMOs, drug and oil companies — 17%   Populism - 17%

His being a weak leader as vice president — 12%
His being very aggressive — 4%   Leadership Style - 16%

His opposition to big tax cuts — 8%   Tax Cuts - 8%

0%   10%   20%   30%   40%

*"Let me read you a list of doubts about Al Gore.
Regardless of how you voted, which THREE describe
the best reasons for not voting for him?"*

November 9, 2000

port for big federal government, support for increased government spending, trusting Washington politicians rather than the people—it was a cluster of things that related to populism.

The role of government is a serious question, and I wish Al Gore was less programmatic in his presentation of what he was for, and more narrative. But there really isn't much difference between Bill Clinton and Al Gore in the policies and levels of spending they want.

But a programmatic narrative gave a sense that it was an accumulation of government programs and government, certainly more than what people were used to. It was not necessarily big spending. Keep in mind, I want to reinforce that we were seen as careful about spending. In any case, it wasn't the main reason we went through this thematic battle. We were attacked on big government, but it didn't affect the vote. The cultural issues did.

The reasons people voted for George Bush? The biggest reasons to vote for George Bush were restoring honor and dignity to the White House, restoring America's military preparedness, and cutting taxes for all taxpayers.

The top two reasons were restoring dignity and honor to the White House, and giving a sense of American strength. These related to the Clinton era, and gave a basis for change in supporting George Bush. We did a regression analysis. It should be noted here for the first time that the pollsters of the two camps had regression models at the same time, saying the same thing.

It would be more alarming if we had regression models saying different things. But when we looked at the range of choices on the various issues, who shares your values was by far the strongest element in predicting people's vote.

The cultural context was obviously a very important piece. When we asked people about this, in the middle of the debates, after two different debates, if you look to the later one, October 9, doubts about Gore saying what people wanted to hear, being too close to Clinton, and not being trustworthy were the top set of the

Reasons to Vote for George W. Bush

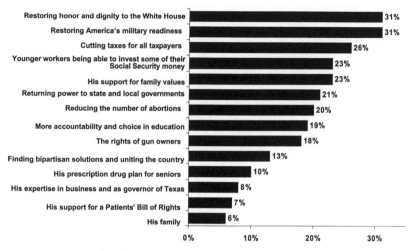

Restoring honor and dignity to the White House	31%
Restoring America's military readiness	31%
Cutting taxes for all taxpayers	26%
Younger workers being able to invest some of their Social Security money	23%
His support for family values	23%
Returning power to state and local governments	21%
Reducing the number of abortions	20%
More accountability and choice in education	19%
The rights of gun owners	18%
Finding bipartisan solutions and uniting the country	13%
His prescription drug plan for seniors	10%
His expertise in business and as governor of Texas	8%
His support for a Patients' Bill of Rights	7%
His family	6%

"Let me read you a list of reasons to vote for George W. Bush. Which THREE best describe the issues and qualities that led you to vote for/consider voting for him?"

November 9, 2000

Predicting the Vote: Issues and Attributes

Variance Explained: 87 Percent

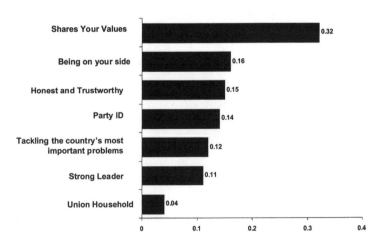

Shares Your Values	0.32
Being on your side	0.16
Honest and Trustworthy	0.15
Party ID	0.14
Tackling the country's most important problems	0.12
Strong Leader	0.11
Union Household	0.04

October 27, 2000

three issues. Clearly, the trust and values things were running together.

We tested after the debates on Al Gore seeming too liberal. We asked, "Let me tell you a few things about Al Gore, and you tell me how reassuring you find these various things." We had two clusters of things.

First, we had a set of things related to family and morality. Gore wanted smaller class sizes where children learn respect and fundamentals. Gore had been married for thirty years. Over 70 percent found that very or somewhat reassuring, and over 40 percent very reassuring. We asked things on government. He has a plan to balance the budget and pay down the national debt. He wants to balance the budget with smaller overall tax cuts so the government does not go back to deficit spending. He is proposing tax cuts for the middle class. He fought for welfare reform and imposed term limits. His efforts to cut government and help bring

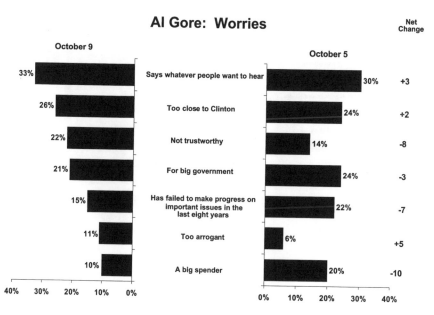

Al Gore: Worries

	October 9		October 5	Net Change
Says whatever people want to hear	33%		30%	+3
Too close to Clinton	26%		24%	+2
Not trustworthy	22%		14%	-8
For big government	21%		24%	-3
Has failed to make progress on important issues in the last eight years	15%		22%	-7
Too arrogant	11%		6%	+5
A big spender	10%		20%	-10

October 9, 2000

the federal government to its lowest level in forty years.

If you really look at the overall numbers on the government re-assurance versus the values reassurance, what voters were look-ing for was to be able to make that decision. To vote for Al Gore was an assurance that he understood, that he was a family person, and they did believe he was a family person. They did believe he was a person with good values. This is not Bill Clinton. This is a period when cultural issues divided the country, and created that 48/48 division.

Let me mention one other thing, which is out of order, but at the end we asked who had the better proposals, Gore or Bush, on education, prescription drugs, seniors, all those things. Some 31 percent who said Gore was better, 19 percent Bush. But half the

Gore Reassurances on Family and Morality

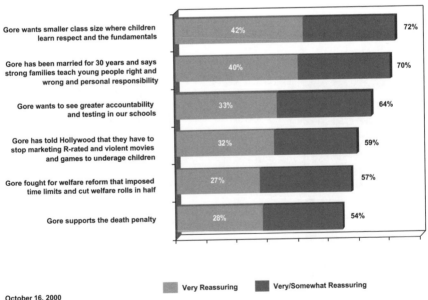

Gore wants smaller class size where children learn respect and the fundamentals	42% — 72%
Gore has been married for 30 years and says strong families teach young people right and wrong and personal responsibility	40% — 70%
Gore wants to see greater accountability and testing in our schools	33% — 64%
Gore has told Hollywood that they have to stop marketing R-rated and violent movies and games to underage children	32% — 59%
Gore fought for welfare reform that imposed time limits and cut welfare rolls in half	27% — 57%
Gore supports the death penalty	28% — 54%

■ Very Reassuring   ■ Very/Somewhat Reassuring

October 16, 2000

sample said it was too confusing to figure out whose proposals were better, or said they both had good proposals or neither had good proposals. They had these battles back and forth on the prescription drugs—too confusing. Half the electorate could not discriminate. That's actually one of the important successes of the Bush campaign. They were able to blur some of these issues.

What I believe is that Al Gore won the election. I know he won the election. I believe that he had a strategy and a campaign that would get him there. We ran in the end of a period in which the cultural forces both took Al Gore and George Bush.

George Bush tried to run as a cultural moderate, a nonthreatening figure. If you really want to understand this electorate, look at people's attitude on choice or on the number of guns they own or

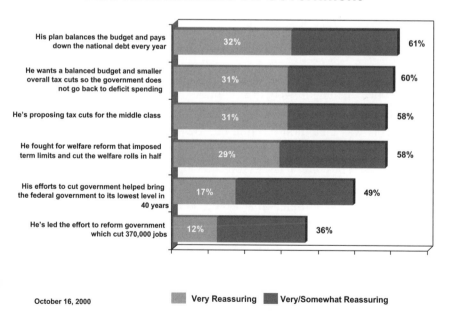

Gore Reassurances on Government

His plan balances the budget and pays down the national debt every year — 32% — 61%

He wants a balanced budget and smaller overall tax cuts so the government does not go back to deficit spending — 31% — 60%

He's proposing tax cuts for the middle class — 31% — 58%

He fought for welfare reform that imposed term limits and cut the welfare rolls in half — 29% — 58%

His efforts to cut government helped bring the federal government to its lowest level in 40 years — 17% — 49%

He's led the effort to reform government which cut 370,000 jobs — 12% — 36%

October 16, 2000

■ Very Reassuring ■ Very/Somewhat Reassuring

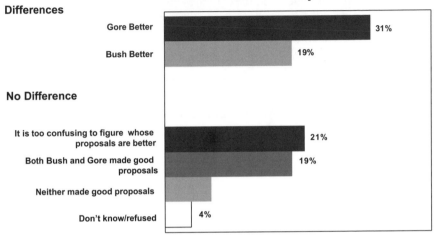

Gore and Bush's Proposals

Differences

Gore Better — 31%

Bush Better — 19%

No Difference

It is too confusing to figure whose proposals are better — 21%

Both Bush and Gore made good proposals — 19%

Neither made good proposals

Don't know/refused — 4%

"Both Al Gore and George W. Bush proposed plans on education, a Patient's Bill of Rights, and prescription drugs for seniors. On these, which of the following is true? "

on other feelings toward Bill Clinton. You can predict the vote with those three things better than anything else.

This was a cultural election that defined George Bush as not moderate on these issues, even though he tried to present himself that way. The cultural issues took Al Gore, who was a family man and a cautious and conservative man of good values who would run a frugal government that would do important things, and we ended up with an evenly divided country because the country is culturally divided.

But that suppressed the majority that was there for Al Gore, and I highlight it because I'm hoping the Democrats build on an understanding of what happened in this election.

EDWARD CARMINES (Indiana University). Neither you nor the two previous Democratic consultants have discussed at great length the preparation of Al Gore to present himself before the public. I think the media have come to a conclusion on this one: that both candidates were flawed in some ways, but that the Republicans did a better job of preparing Bush than the Democrats did of preparing Gore. That Gore was stiff, that he was inconsistent, not just uncomfortable, but he made the voters feel uncomfortable when he came into their living rooms. Can you or Bob Shrum speak to that?

BOB SHRUM (Gore campaign). First of all, I'm reminded by that question of Bobby Kennedy's line when somebody came to him after the '60 election and said, you're a genius. He said, change 60,000 votes and I'm a bum. I suppose the question would be asked in reverse if Gore were sitting in the White House. I think, for example, that George Bush got into some serious trouble in the third debate, and I assume he was very well prepared, but he got into some serious trouble with some of the answers he gave. I think people at very critical moments in the campaign found Al Gore to be a genuine person whom they liked. Now, I agree with Stan. He is not a standard-issue politician. He actually thinks very deeply about these issues. He is, contrary to what was said about him, very unwilling to say things he doesn't believe, and he is not the kind of person you simply hand something to and he goes up and says it. He just doesn't do that. Now, was he prepared? Sure he was prepared. I didn't get into it at length, except to compliment the Bush people on the spin after the first debate, but I thought that Al Gore won the first debate and I thought he won it pretty clearly. I think the second debate as a whole was one of the strangest debates in American political history.

And I think that the numbers bear out the proposition that Al

Gore's acceptance speech may be one of the most successful convention speeches in political history, at least for the voters. I was stunned, listening to reporters afterward who all wanted to say, well gee, he didn't do what he had to do, did he? I mean, boy, that didn't work. He seemed to be talking about too many issues. Except Bernie Shaw, who said, he wasn't sure, that might have been a home run. I think there was an image of Gore as stiff, and so people wanted to see him as stiff. Is Al Gore Mr. Politician? No. Is George W. Bush Mr. Politician? No. But I think the Bush campaign did a very good job of handling whatever problems they felt they had with George W. Bush, and I think Al Gore did a very good job of handling the problems that people had with him.

I traveled with him. Carter and I traded off traveling with him at the end, and he was an extraordinary candidate, especially in those final few weeks. He was an extraordinary candidate in the primaries. Here's a guy who was in deep trouble against Bill Bradley, who was behind in New Hampshire, who, when I said I would go to work for him, a friend of mine in the press corps took me to dinner and said, "Please, don't do this, it's gonna ruin your reputation, he's gonna lose in the primary." Instead, he became the only modern candidate in history in a seriously contested primary situation, to win every primary. Had we been given the victory I think we won, maybe I'd be answering the question in reverse, or maybe poor McKinnon would have to answer it in reverse.

GREENBERG. Basically likeability came out fairly even between the two campaigns. We drove George Bush up as unfavorable through the last few weeks, but the two candidates ended up at a comparable place. When we did lose ground in the first debate, a lot of it was stylistic. I'd say half of it was stylistic and half of it was playing on the trust exaggeration that came after the fact. There was a fallback, particularly with women voters, after the first debate, and we had to work to bring that back.

FRED STEEPER (Bush campaign). Stan, the numbers you're posting, as well as the ones you've just showed here, showed a tighter national race and a more consistent national race and even maybe an aggregation of national polls. The first question is, did you see, and did the Gore campaign really acknowledge, a closing in the last ten days favorable to Gore? The second question is about Ralph Nader. Was it a concerted strategy on the part of the Gore campaign to aggressively go after and challenge Nader voters, ask them why they were wasting their votes? Just as an editorial comment, I never saw a candidate get so much attention bemoaning his lack of attention in the last couple of weeks as Ralph Nader. At the time I thought, what are they doing? They're talking about Nader, but was that a concerted effort or was it press driven?

GREENBERG. Let me deal with the first question. Democracy Corps polls were published. Democracy Corps polling at the end was half a point or a point difference between the candidates. But the Democracy Corps was weekly. We were polling nationally, three samples a week, in the Gore campaign. The pattern we found was that we had lost our lead after the first debate and then we continued to slip, so that at our lowest point, about a week after the first debate, we were down about 3 points. Then we began to move back up. It was not one moment. We began to move up steadily.

You could see it in the polls. We began to move up steadily at the end, until our last polls were either even or a point ahead. I think what happened in the end was the undecided broke two to one against us.

There was only 3 percent undecided. Two to one against us, and the Nader voters who decided broke two to one for us, and balanced out and we ended up with a slight win. On the network polls, there is a job to do, and I'm sure it's going to be done, because there is a process in which the national polls, because they fear being caught up in the variation of polls on a given day, apply party weights.

SHRUM. Stan became funny in our campaign. Over the last two weeks, Carter and Daley would meet Stan one week and then the next week, Daley and I would meet Stan as we traded off traveling with the candidate. We'd look at Stan and he'd say, no change. Stan had a remarkably stable pattern the last two weeks. The question was, "What were the Nader people going to do and what were the undecided people going to do?" The CBS poll, which restrained itself in New Hampshire and didn't end up in the wrong place (unlike lots of other people in the New Hampshire primary) I wouldn't criticize. But there was a general tendency, especially with the CNN poll and the Battleground poll, to have huge massive unexplained shifts in one day, which the Bush people must have found amusing, too. One morning, Tad Devine said, "I wonder if 19 million people got up this morning and changed their minds about who they were gonna vote for for president?"

KATHLEEN FRANKOVIC (CBS News). I have to concur with you. There is definitely a story waiting to be written about tracking polls in this campaign, which because of the nature of tracking polls, and because of the journalistic value system of reporting what you have, you can't hold back once it is set in motion. It did show some very odd and peculiar movements that were the function of a number of things, of the small samples and the reporting on a daily basis, the function of likely voter models developed to use at the end of the campaign, but being applied throughout the campaign, and in some cases that put equal weight on whether you're paying as much attention to the campaign as to other questions, including past voting behavior, which showed a lot more movement than surveys conducted in a finite amount of time and done occasionally. But that's a different issue from the issue of party weighting. In theory, CNN and *USA Today* did not do party weighting, though it sometimes happens.

SHRUM. They just did something weird.

FRANKOVIC. There was a huge difference, yes.

GREENBERG. I watched Frank Newport of Gallup go on TV with a straight face and say the reason for this variation is because the voters change their minds from day to day. I will get you the quotes.

FRANKOVIC. I'm not going to contest that.

GREENBERG. The reason for this Gallup report was not their party weights and not their turnout models, it was that voters were fickle. Now, we did one thing in this election in addition to our overall tracking. Our overall tracking at the end of the last two weeks showed the race even, Gore a point ahead. The network tracking, on average, moved toward being even. It was never even on average. If you took all the public polls, they averaged out at around a 3-point advantage for Bush. However, we took our state polls and every available public poll, and any candidate poll we could get, and created a national model based on the state polls. It came out to almost even. The reason, I believe, is that people were not applying either party weights or turnout models to the state polls in the same way that the networks were doing.

In any case, there is a process of disclosure that needs to happen on these public polls, because it led to a very misleading view of the world. On the question of the Nader voters, which I didn't answer, I was very focused on the Nader voters. We did panel surveys back to Nader voters, and we found that the two issues on which Nader voters would switch were on choice and the environment. But they believed they didn't have to, because Nader voters were very antipolitical. They had doubts about Gore as authentic and real and could rationalize their vote. But on choice, they thought he was pro-choice and they thought for sure that George Bush would appoint a Supreme Court nominee that would threaten the right to choose.

The second issue was the environment. Nader voters did think that Al Gore believed in that, there was conviction, and that Bush had a record of threat. So we ran direct mail and radio advertising very heavily, in Oregon in particular, and special surveys. I didn't expect to win Oregon in the end. I think the reason we did was the directed campaign there and in parts of Wisconsin.

SHRUM. By the way, the one argument that did not work against Nader voters was to insult them and tell them, "Don't waste your vote." The argument that worked and that we tried to make, was the fundamental choices on the environment and on a woman's right to choose, and that the right way to make those choices was to vote for Al Gore.

But if you said to people, "Don't be dumb and waste your vote," you lost Nader voters.

I don't believe that when traveling around you necessarily see a lot, because you can always get big crowds in advance. In the second to last week, we went to a rally in Madison, Wisconsin, where our polling had not been particularly good, and Nader had been getting a lot of support. The crowd was so massive that it not only filled the square in front of the State House, it filled the streets that radiated out from the State House. I called Stan afterward and said, "Something is happening here in Wisconsin." It was young people. We could begin to see it in the response we were getting in the streets, but it was not because anyone said

Ralph Nader was a bad guy, or, you're dumb if you vote for Ralph Nader.

ELIHU KATZ (University of Pennsylvania). As I understand it, your argument is about the salience of cultural issues. If so, are cultural issues on your list of issues?

Second, are you measuring salience? Third, you haven't given us any data of changes over time, either on the issues or on their salience. Fourth, if you knew it during the campaign, was anything done about it? This is, you say, not retrospective.

GREENBERG. First of all, in the table I presented earlier, you have at the bottom "shares your values" and "addressing the moral problems facing the country," so that actually the classical one used "on your side" is caught up with lots of issues of that. It's advocacy for people, but it's also whether you understand their lives and respect their values. It was measured throughout, and it was very important to us at the convention. It was important to the whole tone of the convention, which talked about family. It was important to the biography. There were ads that ran throughout the entire month of August to Labor Day.

We ran a whole series of spots that were labeled cultural values. I don't know what they were called when they actually ran, but there was a whole series of spots on cultural values.

That's why we're using the regression model to show that "shares your values" had more than two and a half times the predictive power as the next highest element. I don't know how else to measure salience. I have tracked "shares your values" over time. Democrats used to have the advantage on it. They lost it during the impeachment battle and did not have it going into the '98 elections or going into this election. So it was an important thing to address in this election. People wanted to hear more about it, but we were always in the process of addressing it.

KATHLEEN HALL JAMIESON (University of Pennsylvania). I'd like to ask whether you agree across the campaigns about the effect, if any, of the network call of the election for George W. Bush. That is, is there evidence that it created a presumption that he already was the president in the minds of voters?

SHRUM. I have no evidence one way or another, about the effect of that night.

GREENBERG. Had the election night ended up inconclusive, with no call, and Florida in doubt, I believe the entire Florida recount would have played out differently. There was an impatience with Gore that actually lessened. It was related to the presumption that George Bush had somehow won or been deemed the legitimate president-elect. So I do think the call had a major impact on the coverage, and on voter presumptions, as they wanted to throw up their hands. It was obvious that Al Gore should be the one who bows out. I think it was a major factor in the recount process.

SHRUM. It was especially a factor at the beginning of the recount process, when there was the feeling of "Why is he doing this?" Toward the end of the recount process, almost counterintuitively, there was more patience with what he was doing, and I think that was a very honest answer to say there's no evidence one way or the other.

Impressionistically, my sense is that it made a big difference that Dan Rather said, "Let's give a big hearty Texas welcome to the new president of the United States, George W. Bush," and all these explosions went off and everything else. Then twenty minutes later, they had to come back and say, "Well now wait a minute. We're not sure. Gore is contesting this." Let me put it this way. I don't have any evidence, but if you guys want to go back and rerun the film of history and swap places on that call, I'd be glad to do it.

GREENBERG. Kathleen, is your question whether or not the early call or the late call affected voter perceptions that day?

JAMIESON. No, the question is, did the call of the presidency for Bush, the second call of Florida for the evening that was then retracted, create a presumption on the part of voters that basically Gore hadn't won and was now trying to get something that he didn't deserve? Is there any polling evidence on either side that would help us answer that question?

GREENBERG. I think Bob and Fred are right. I don't think the voters tuned into that. A month after the election, if you polled them again, they still thought the race was dead even a month after the election. There were polls done after the election. It had to do with media perception and it made it very difficult for the Gore campaign in those thirty days, because they were now fighting against a presumption that already was stated.

SHRUM. That part I agree with. I do think voters paid attention that night, actually.

GREENBERG. Totally paid attention.

SHRUM. I think people thought that George Bush was president. We thought George Bush was president. I mean, Al Gore was walking into the War Memorial and was not going to go to the holding room. He was going straight to the stage to give a concession speech and without telling the poor guy who was in charge of him, we said, get him on a phone, take him to the holding room. He said, I don't want to go to the holding room. And we said, take him to the holding room. So he went to the holding room. And then we told him what was going on. The thing that always amazes me, by the way, about that night, that I've never heard an answer to, is how suddenly Bush went to a 50,000 vote lead in Florida at 98.5 percent, or 98.4 percent. Then three-tenths of a point later he was at a 1,500-vote lead.

Four

Kathleen Frankovic

Kathleen Frankovic is director of surveys and producer for CBS News. She is also CBS News representative to the Board of Managers of the Voter News Service. She was one of the authors of the special report on CBS News election night coverage and is president-elect of the World Association of Public Opinion Researchers, and past president of the American Association for Public Opinion Research. She holds a Ph.D. in political science from Rutgers University and has taught at the University of Vermont. She is an analyst of elections as well as a pollster, and a contributor to Gerald Pomper's volumes on presidential elections, including The Election of 2000.

I have to tell you that the morning of the election, when we released our last poll number, my hugest fear was that I would have to spend the next four years explaining why our preelection poll was 10 points off or something horrible like that.

It turned out that the final preelection poll numbers we released had Al Gore up by 1 point over George W. Bush, and that 1 point was actually a function of rounding. If you look at it to the tenth of a decimal point, our poll had Gore up over Bush nationally by half a percentage point. So, I feel pretty good about that. Of course, was I surprised at the end of election night to discover that I am probably going to be spending the next four years explaining something.

However, the networks were not the only ones with problems on election night and Election Day. The five weeks after the election, before a president was named, exposed a lot of flaws in the American electoral system. Things that might only have been known to election officials and party officials are now known to a lot more people. Yesterday's *Washington Post* had an article exposing flaws in other models; it was referred to earlier as "political scientists apologize for the failures of models that had worked for many elections in predicting the outcome, and gave different explanations for why they didn't work this year."

I know that my responsibility is to talk about election night, but I want to say a few things first about the nature of the electorate and the nature of this election. I wrote a chapter for *The Election of 2000* on election trends with Monika McDermott, who was the manager of surveys at CBS News this election year and is now the associate director of the Eagleton Poll at Rutgers University. We confirmed a lot of what the analysts said this morning. For example, American voters judged the economy to be in the best shape in more than a decade, yet they were unsure how much credit the incumbent administration deserved. In fact, the percentage of people who told us they thought that the Republicans in Congress were largely responsible for the state of the economy was about the same as the percentage who said that the Clinton administration was. So in this election, the underlying question for the campaign was what the good economy meant. Voters also expressed very conflicted and ambivalent attitudes toward the role of government. While in principle, a majority favored smaller government, large majorities favored expanded government actions in a variety of areas: health care, prescription drugs, education. Even among those who favored smaller government, large numbers favored increased government action in at least some areas.

Kathleen Frankovic. Photo by Kyle Cassidy.

An unusual issue for pollsters in 2000 was figuring out the real meaning of voters' feelings about President Clinton. There was an incumbent vice president who—like other vice presidents before him—could emerge as an individual only after his convention. However, because of the strategy of the Republican opponent, Al Gore did not have the traditional Democratic issue advantage.

I want to note a couple of things about the candidates and their role in this process. Both of the major party candidates were tied to presidents: Gore to Clinton, and George W. Bush to his father. In the summer of 1999, we asked people what came to mind when they heard the name George W. Bush. About one in five told us "the President." So there was a little bit of confusion there. It went away within a couple of months, but the most popular answer even in the fall of 1999 when people were asked "What do you think of when you hear the name George W. Bush" was "Son of a president." It took a long time for George W. Bush to become identified on his own.

In both parties, the voters ended up choosing fairly traditional candidates and avoiding candidates perceived as likely to have new ideas. They chose candidates who they believed would follow familiar approaches to get things done. The candidates themselves had many similarities by the time the campaign was over. Apart from Gore's problems on questions of pandering and saying what he thought people wanted to hear, and Bush's problems regarding his perceived lack of preparedness for the White House and inexperience in foreign policy, the differences between the two candidates were very small on a whole host of candidate characteristics. About seven in ten voters said both candidates shared their moral values. About six in ten said both candidates had the skills to work with members of both parties. About seven in ten said both candidates had strong qualities of leadership, and although more said that Gore cared about people like themselves, a majority said the same thing about Bush. Both candidates had weaknesses. There were doubts about whether either man could be trusted to keep his word, and doubts about whether they would keep their campaign promises. In many ways, the candidates were shockingly alike.

After the Democratic convention, Gore emerged with the highest bounce ever for a Democratic candidate. In fact, the only candidate who exceeded Gore's convention bounce was George Bush in 1988, who went from 17 points back to 6 points ahead. In our polling, Gore went from about 11 points back before the convention to 1 point ahead afterward. After the convention, negative evaluations of Gore dropped and positive evaluations rose. The debates—unfortunately, from Gore's point of view—actually brought back some of the negatives he had managed to wipe out at the Democratic convention. But by the time the campaign was over, both candidates had just about the same number of people with favorable evaluations of them. That helps to explain why we ended up with such a close race.

Another point about this campaign that surprises people—it certainly surprised me, and it may be testimony to the job the campaigns did and the kind of campaigns they ran—was that in our polls, voter satisfaction with the choices this year was the highest it had ever been since we started asking that question in 1980. A clear majority said that they were generally satisfied with the choices they had in this election. There have been other elections where voters were satisfied. They were evenly divided in 1980, 1984, 1992, and 1996. And they were highly *dissatisfied* in 1988. But in 2000 more than 60 percent said they were satisfied with the choices they had. So from a polling standpoint, voter satisfaction, confusion over the role of the economy, and split opinions about the incumbent president are what led to the electoral ambivalence that we saw on election day. No single issue dominated the reasons people gave for why they voted as they did.

There was one quality that dominated in another exit poll question: honesty. That factor certainly helped George W. Bush.

Voters sometimes give different answers depending on the question they are asked. Every time we asked people if what mattered more to them in choosing a president was a candidate's issue positions or a candidate's personal characteristics, issues won. People who claimed that issues mattered more were more likely to say they were voting for Gore. The people who said personal qualities mattered more were more likely to say they were voting for Bush. In fact, there were more "personal quality" voters who said they were voting for Bush than "issues" voters who said they were voting for Gore. But if you asked the question a different way, you saw issues diminish in concern and importance. We asked, "What matters more, a candidate agreeing with you on important policies, a candidate's honesty, or a candidate's leadership?" Given that choice, only 7 percent chose policy agreement and four out of ten opted for honesty, with a similar answer for leadership, each something that could be labeled a "presidential quality."

I don't want to make it appear that honesty—which dominated the qualities that voters cared about—led directly to the Bush showing in this election. During the course of the election, the point was frequently made that while Americans thought the country was on the right track generally, a majority also thought that when it came to moral things, the country was on the wrong track. We've heard about moral issues and morality as factors in the campaign. What was interesting on Election Day is that even those people who said they cared about morality, who said that they thought that this was a problem, weren't necessarily driven by it. When they answered the question "What's more important in a president, being a good manager or being a person of high moral standards?" on the exit poll, being a good manager was the more popular choice even among those people who said morality was important to them.

It's important to note that it wasn't just the electorate overall that was evenly split. Some of these issues affected voters as individuals. Individual voters were ambivalent about what they really wanted. Asking people questions in different ways revealed that to us throughout the campaign, and certainly on Election Day. On Election Day, what did most voters want? Many wanted a smaller government that does a lot of things. Many conflicted voters who wanted a smaller government nevertheless favored additional government involvement in either education or in providing prescription drugs. That might have been where the election was decided, because among those conflicted people, Bush had a small edge.

This is important because the discussion and the debate since the election has highlighted partisan divisions. Polls conducted after the election but while counts were going on in Florida, indicated that a lot of people who supported one candidate would not view the other candidate's election as legitimate. We could see people were a lot more divided and polarized in attitudes about the candidates after the election than before the election. Al Gore's favorable ratings dropped dramatically in the course of the challenge, only to come back toward the end and certainly jump up after his concession speech in December. But all of that, and all of the drama of election night, and the drama of the ensuing few weeks, seems to have made people forget what really was there during the election.

So much for the campaign and the election. Let me talk now about what took place on election night. I'll be fairly general, but hopefully I'll give you enough information. In the course of helping put together the CBS report, I discovered a historical fact that surprised me no end. In 1964, in the California Republican primary, CBS News projected that Barry Goldwater would win the state of California and all its delegates at the Republican convention at 7:22 P.M. Pacific Standard Time. The polls had closed in Los Angeles, but the polls would not close in the San Francisco area for another thirty-eight minutes. And that early call was a call that engendered discussion and debate similar to what we've seen happen in this election.

CBS has been developing its system of making calls on election night for a long time. In 1964, Lou Harris was involved, but it's fair to say that the decision system that is in use now is much like what emerged late in 1968, although the procedure has been modified in many ways. Once the polls have closed, we enter data from sample precincts into a variety of estimators, that is, a variety of statistical models that look at the pattern of votes precinct by precinct, and the size of the vote. Estimates of turnout are stratified by geographic region and by party strength in those precincts. Then, using either a simple estimate or a ratio estimate looking at past behavior, we make estimates of the likely outcome in a state. Since the 1980s, exit poll data collected throughout the day have been entered into similar models. Turnout estimates and vote tabulations are also collected on a precinct-by-precinct basis so that one can understand and analyze what happens.

Since the 1960s there has been a "decision desk" at CBS, usually headed by a CBS executive. It consists of a number of election experts and statisticians who are evaluating the models and the quality control procedures. In some cases they look at data precinct by precinct, making judgments based on reports of how difficult this information was to collect, looking at the models and waiting for a confidence level that justifies making a call. That call is sent to the graphic systems that display it on air and to a producer who passes the information along to the individuals who make the call on the air. That procedure was used at CBS prior to the formation of both Voter Research and Surveys and Voter News Service. It still is.

Ben Wattenberg, one of the authors of the CNN Report, wrote an article about a week and a half after election day and before the CNN committee he served on was announced, in which he asked a question that a lot of people might have been asking on election night: "What is the VNS?" That column was written before he said the networks needed to have their wrists slapped with a machete. The Voter News Service is a product of a little bit of consolidation and a little bit of hard reality. After the 1988 election, it was clear that individual networks would no longer be able to support the huge amount of manpower and cost required to have individual data collection systems on election day. In fact, at least one network shut down its election unit.

Networks had cooperated before. In fact, prior to 1964, networks actually counted the vote themselves. This required stationing reporters in tens of thousands of precincts nationwide—an enormous operation for one night's work. The networks combined to form the News Election Service to collect the vote from all precincts and counties nationwide and then transmit those totals to their clients, then the three broadcast networks and two wire services, AP and UPI.

After the 1988 election, it seemed to make sense to consolidate the entire Election Day data-gathering operation. So Voter Research and Surveys was formed by the three broadcast networks plus CNN to conduct exit polls on Election Day, and collect votes from sample precincts in all the states. Before VRS was formed, CBS did not do exit polls in every state. The formation of VRS gave us the capacity to collect and see more data on Election Day. Voter Research and Surveys continued through two national elections. Not only did it collect the data, but it took responsibility for reviewing the models and making recommendations to the members as to when a race in each state could be called, including all major statewide races and House races nationally in all presidential and off-year elections.

After the 1992 election, Voter Research and Surveys was merged with NES, the News Election Service, to create Voter News Service, or VNS, in order to combine all Election Day data-gathering operations into one place. As I noted, the underlying models remained, though they had been adapted and changed since the late 1960s. In the 1994 election, ABC chose not to rely on VNS' call recommendations, but instead brought in its own decision team and made calls in critical Senate races and governors' races before other member organizations. Some of that was probably done simply by reallocating resources: more people looking at the most important decision screens. By doing that, ABC changed the rules. After the 1994 election, every member of VNS established its own decision operation, with additional consultants to look through the data and make calls on their own timetable when they felt the data justified them.

The CBS decision team consisted of individuals who had long histories with CBS and VRS and, in fact, VNS too. They had intimate knowledge about the data collection process and the decision screens. They were shared with CNN and physically located somewhere in the CBS building, though not in the CBS studio. This system was in place on election night, and is responsible for many of the calls that CBS News and CNN made on election night. I say "many" because a lot of the calls, particularly a lot of the easy poll-closing calls, were made by VNS, which maintained its own decision team.

So on Election Day, we had a data collection process in all fifty states and the District of Columbia, involving about 1,400 exit poll precincts and close to 5,000 sample precincts. There were sample precincts in all of the states and the District of Columbia, as well as county vote tabulation, which takes place throughout the country, gathering data, for the most part, from county election officials. We started looking at all this information at 1:00 in the afternoon, when we begin to receive exit poll data. The news organizations can examine decision management screens that describe every precinct: its vote report, issues with data collection at the precincts—are the interviewers having trouble with the election officials, are they required to stand far away—are there weather conditions in some states that might affect the quality of the data, and so forth. The interviewer is not just handing out questionnaires to voters, but he or she is also noting for those voters who won't fill out the questionnaire or are otherwise missed three facts: their gender, race, and apparent age (we have three categories: under thirty, over sixty, and everybody in between). This process, as I said, began at 1:00 in the afternoon. Studio personnel were in place around 5:00 or 5:30. The *Evening News* at CBS starts at 6:30, preceded by a special report at 6:00, when Kentucky and Indiana closed. At 7:00, we went on the air with our election night coverage—a special report that would continue until it was all over. In reality, it ended *before* it was over, but we did stay on the air continuously until 7 A.M. when the *Early Show* came on. The correspondents in the studio did an insert at seven o'clock in the *Early Show*. They then went away briefly but came back at nine o'clock to do it again. I spent many days—not just election night, but many days afterward—in the control room, as we tried to keep track of all the various counts and countercounts in Florida.

At 7:00 P.M. on Tuesday, November 7, the vast majority of Florida's polls closed. They closed in those counties that make up 95 percent of the voting-age population. The data from the exit poll does not show a call status in the race. The model includes exit poll interviews from forty-four of the forty-five surveyed precincts that had reported in. They showed a small lead for Gore. At about 7:40 P.M., the computations from VNS of the various models (and there were about ten of them) did show a call status in the Florida presidential race. That meant that, statistically, Gore was leading. He was leading at a level of confidence of 99.5 percent, but a call still wasn't made.

At 7:45, the analysts looked more closely at the data, as they had other pieces of information they could use, such as actual vote totals from sample precincts in Kentucky, which had been called at 6:00 P.M. for George W. Bush. When votes from sample precincts came from the exact same precincts where the exit poll was conducted, you can compare the actual vote within that precinct to what the survey indicated. The system does a computation to check if there is any survey bias in those precincts, from the data collection, the interviewing process, the surveying and sampling process at the precinct level. Kentucky is the only state we have this for at 7:45 P.M. Indiana had also closed at six o'-clock, but Indiana is very slow to count, so there was not enough data in from sample precincts to do that computation in Indiana.

In Kentucky, what is most interesting is that the exit poll seems to have overstated Bush's lead. That is, the sampling at the polling places overstated Bush's percentage, according to the survey bias computation. That's an interesting piece of information, but still nobody calls the race. At the same time, the tabulated vote is being reported, and while only about 4 percent of the precincts statewide have reported in—this is forty-five minutes after the polls close in 95 percent of the state—the calculation done off the tabulated vote also indicates a Gore lead. That doesn't just mean he's ahead in the vote counted so far, it means that given their location within the state, projecting to the other parts of the state, it means that Gore is actually ahead statewide.

The first computation of the within-precinct error from Florida came in. Once enough precincts that were both surveyed precincts and sample precincts reported, like the Kentucky computation, it suggested that the exit poll was overstating the Bush vote in Florida. So, at 7:50—actually we know from our broadcast time, that it was 7:50 and 11 seconds—CBS called Gore the winner in Florida, 9 minutes and 50 seconds before the polls closed in the Panhandle counties. The other networks called Florida a few minutes before or after that. VNS called Florida at 7:52, as did the AP. *Everyone* was looking at these data, at these computations, and *everyone* came to the same conclusion. It was a very, very clear conclusion.

The Gore call stood for about two hours before it was retracted. But let me say some things now about why that call was made, and what we know now about the system and the problems. The statistical computations look at past votes, make ratio comparisons between current vote and past vote (there are data from a number of past elections entered into the system), and choose an election for comparison based on the correlation with a prior vote. In this election, between 7:40 and 7:50, the highest correlation was between the Bush vote this year and Jeb Bush's vote in 1998. The correlation, precinct by precinct, compared this year and two years ago, was about .91. That was higher than any other correlation between any other candidate and past vote. What that did in the ratio estimator was to make an assumption about the level of absentee votes, putting them at approximately what they had been in 1998. In 1998, about 8 percent of the vote was cast absentee in Florida, and that was built into the model. In Florida, traditionally, the absentee vote is much more Republican than the vote at the precincts on Election Day. This year, it was about 20 points more Republican than Election Day voters. So the size of the absentee vote was a major concern.

There was another election for which the correlations were quite high, and if you were to average the correlations between the Democratic vote and the Republican vote, it was actually a stronger correlation than the '98 election. That was the 1996 presidential election. The correlation between the Bush vote in 2000, precinct by precinct, and the Dole vote in 1996 was about .87 or .88. The correlation of the Gore vote with the Clinton vote in '96 was about .8. The correlation of the Gore vote and the Democratic candidate's vote in the '98 gubernatorial election was only .7. So, on average, 1996 was the better race for the model. And had the model selected that race, it would have used the absentee vote total in 1996, which was 10 percent of the total vote. Just making that change in the ratio estimator would have meant that the race would not have reached "call" status and we wouldn't have called it. That was one of three problems with the Florida Gore call.

The second problem was that it looks as if the survey sampling error at 7:50 P.M. was probably an artifact of the time of day. By the end of the night, the overestimate of Bush by the survey in the individual precincts had disappeared. If we had that piece of information at 7:50 P.M., we might not have made the Gore call.

The final problem was the total exit poll precinct sampling error. The exit poll sample contains 45 precincts, a subsample of the 120 precincts that make up the total sample precincts. The 120 precincts in total were almost dead-on in estimating the final outcome. But the 45 exit poll precincts were not as accurate a sample.

We retracted the call for Gore based on information we began receiving after nine o'clock, when one of the estimators—the one based on the tabulated county vote—showed a Bush lead. This was a change. Up till then, everything indicated a Gore win. The problem was magnified by a report of vote data from Duval County that turned out to be wrong. It was an entry mistake that overstated Gore by a huge amount. And it certainly seemed to support the accuracy of a Gore win in the tabulated votes. This error was discovered about thirty minutes later and was deleted from the system. At that point it became clear that we might have a problem. It was not at all clear who had won in Florida, but it was clear that we couldn't stand behind the Gore call. So at 9:54, we withdrew the call. CBS was in a seven-minute local cutaway, which our affiliates use for their local election reporting, and which occur at 23 past the hour and then again at 53 past the hour. So I had that time to walk into the studio and, along with the News Division president, tell Dan Rather we were retracting Florida. We made that retraction on-air at 10 P.M. I think there were a lot of other network retractions happening at about the same time.

I note the Duval County issue specifically because the retraction probably might have been made a little bit earlier had it not been for that error, but maybe not. There were other things, and other data in the system that suggested the call for Gore was correct.

Looking at the coverage and at how CBS News at least was reporting the outcome, we showed the popular vote about fifteen times between 7 and 11 P.M. Every time we showed the popular vote nationwide, George W. Bush was way ahead. Remember, the states that close early are states that tend to be Republican. It gives Republican candidates an opportunity to amass electoral votes a whole lot earlier than Democrats do. From 7 to 11 P.M., there were only two short periods, totaling 46 minutes, when Al Gore led in the electoral vote. For the rest of the time, George W. Bush was ahead. We showed or talked about the electoral vote over one hundred times in that period, and Bush was ahead the vast majority of those times.

So that gets us through the problems with the Florida call. The within-precinct sample, the overall exit poll precinct sample, the model's choice of a past race—which seemed reasonable on its face—added to the problem. Just like when a plane crashes, it's never because of one thing. It is a variety of things that all seem to happen at once.

Let me move on to what happened beginning at about 2:00 in the morning, when there were relatively few states left uncalled, including Oregon, Wisconsin, and Iowa. There wasn't much to be settled at this point, and it became clear that the Florida outcome (and its twenty-five electoral votes) was going to determine who won. Al Gore couldn't win without it, although at that point, George W. Bush could. At about 2 A.M., the decision team started looking closely at the Bush margin in the Florida popular vote. The VNS count, which comes from county election officials, gave him about a 29,000-vote lead. There were still votes in some very strongly Democratic counties that had yet to come in: Miami-Dade, Broward, Palm Beach. The Associated Press was also collecting tabulated votes at this point—something they have been doing independently for decades. The Associated Press numbers showed less of a Bush lead, but we weren't looking at them. We learned after the election that the AP feed, which is supposed to be integrated with the VNS feed at VNS, somehow didn't work, and so VNS didn't have the Associated Press numbers. I should note that VNS historically has had decent quality control, but had we known that VNS was without the AP numbers, it might have affected the way we went about calling the race. Our decision team members might have been checking AP numbers themselves. They could be gotten off the computer system off the Web, or from our in-house AP feed.

At 2:05 A.M., we were showing a Bush lead in Florida of about 29,000 votes. The end-of-night estimation model projected a small Bush lead, but nobody wanted to call this state, which would decide the election, on anything except absolute assurance that this was right. At 2:09 A.M., numbers came in from Volusia County. I don't know how much you know about the Volusia County problem, but it's a wonderful example of election problems that need to be fixed at the county and the precinct levels. I remember on election night somebody said, "Why is it taking them so long to count the votes" and I told them, "It's hard to count votes. This is a system that works only intermittently. In many places, we're not talking about professional election officials. The workers come in only on Election Day. There are multiple mechanisms that differ from county to county. It's hard, and it can be wrong."

Volusia County includes Daytona Beach, and Volusia County has centrally counted precincts. In other words, the precinct computer voting cards are taken to a central location and counted there. When precinct 216 from DeLand came in, somehow or other, this precinct, which only has about 100 voters, registered a count of more than 500 for Bush and *minus* 16,000 for Al Gore. Gore's vote total went *down*. But this wasn't immediately noticed.

The Volusia County counting system had had problems earlier that day. It needed to be zeroed out at one point. At another point, it counted 9,000 votes for the Socialist Worker Party candidate. These were real problems. They fixed them by the end of the night, but there were real problems.

This counting error happened shortly after midnight and made its way into the AP totals. It didn't go into the VNS totals until about 2:09 A.M. It was verified with the county official. At this point, Bush's VNS statewide lead increased to more than 51,000 votes. That was when the CBS News decision desk seriously started to consider calling the state for Bush. The question was, where were the outstanding votes, how many were there, and were they going to be enough for Gore to overcome Bush's lead? The outstanding votes were mainly from Dade and Palm Beach and Broward, which are strong Democratic counties. The decision desk did the calculation. Even assuming that we were going to see huge margins for Gore in the outstanding counties, it appeared that Bush's margin would still be greater than 30,000 at the end of the night.

It turned out that there were a couple of other errors in the system. Brevard County briefly undercounted Gore's votes by 4,000. That error was still in the system. That meant we had 20,000 missing Gore votes. In addition, the calculations of the yet-to-be counted votes in some counties was underestimated, because the VNS expected that the precincts yet to report were, on average, approximately the same size as the precincts that had reported. It turned out that there were some large precincts included in the unreporting precincts in Palm Beach County and some absentee votes that people thought had been counted that were not. That meant that a larger number of votes than estimated had yet to be counted.

At 2:16 in the morning—after Fox and NBC called Florida and the election for Bush—the AP corrected the Volusia County vote. There was a statewide 17,000-vote drop, to a 30,000-vote Bush lead down from 50,000 before. But we didn't see the AP correction. In fact, at 2:17—actually at 2:17:52—CBS called Florida, and the election, for Bush.

HENRY BRADY (University of California). I want to go through some quick math here with respect to the early call in the Panhandle. There are about 6 million voters in Florida; 95 percent are outside the Panhandle. So 5 percent of 6 million is 300,000. It's the last ten minutes. How long are the polls open in Florida?

FRANKOVIC. It's at least twelve hours. It might be thirteen.

BRADY. So something like 1/60 of the voters might vote in that period, and I get 5,000 people.

FRANKOVIC. Eighteen percent of the vote that was cast in the Panhandle was cast absentee.

BRADY. So it would be less than 5,000. So 4,000 people might plausibly have voted in those last ten minutes. How many of those probably heard the call?

FRANKOVIC. I have no data.

BRADY. I'm just trying to get some idea of why people are concerned about the Panhandle. This math suggests to me there's just not enough people.

If half of the 4,000 people heard it, that's 2,000. How many people might be affected? The biggest prediction we had out there is John Jackson's, which is around 10 percent, so that might be 400 voters difference, and maybe that's enough to make people concerned, but it's not a big effect. And that's really making, I think, strong assumptions about how people might be affected.

FRANKOVIC. A week after the election, a couple of Associated Press stories reported on one group's plan to sue the networks on this. It quoted three election officials in three of the counties, who uniformly said "What? Nothing happened. People didn't walk out." You made an assumption, about the equal distribution of vote at the precinct level throughout the day, but historically, the majority—about 60 percent—of the vote at the precinct level is cast before noon local time.

BRADY. So the biggest we could get might be 100 to 200 voters. The absolute biggest.

KARL ROVE (Bush campaign). First of all, it's extraordinary that we're sitting here saying that at worst, we may have only a 5 percent impact. The election was decided by 537 votes. Second, CBS was not the first to call. If you look at the eastern part of the Panhandle, turnout was 69 or 70 percent. If you look at the western part of the Panhandle, which is in the Central time zone, turnout was 63 percent. I don't think there is a big difference between the people who live in the eastern part of northern Florida and the people who live in the western part of northern Florida. If you look at adjoining counties on either side of the Central/Eastern time zone line, there was a difference in the amount of turnout. So those early calls had an impact. If you don't want to consider Florida, consider the rest of the country.

When the trifecta—Michigan, Pennsylvania, and Florida—were called, there were 113 Electoral College votes still at stake in states ranging from Iowa to Alaska and Hawaii. Iowa votes until 10:00 P.M. Eastern Standard Time, for example. So there was a considerable amount of time in which votes could have been affected. Turnout improved 2.1 percent nationwide in every state in the 113 Electoral College votes that were still open. Only two states were at or above the national average in improvement. Every other state was below and, in fact, a great many of them had negative numbers, or lower turnout in 2000 than in 1996. Either the media have an impact or they don't. If media have no impact, then why report? If they do have an impact, why not care deeply about the potential impact on the margin? A study by John Lott suggests that as many as 15,000 votes were affected in the Panhandle.

Whether it is 5,000 or 15,000, why has the media's role in the process gone from passive observer to active participant—and with a deleterious effect on the outcome?

CURTIS GANS (Committee for the Study of the American Electorate). The central question is why are you not reporting the results? Why are you making declarations? In Florida, there was only one piece of reportable news that night that had actual effect, and that was the tabulated result. That's what determines who wins. You may have errors along the way, but that final count is the only thing that determines who wins. If you just reported that, you'd never get it wrong and you'd never be premature.

The error was not only in Florida. New Mexico and Washington also had to be retracted, and Virginia and Georgia and a couple of other states were really one-sided states that the media's data showed as too close to call.

BILL KNAPP (Gore campaign). I don't know if it would have made a difference in Florida, but that's neither our position nor the networks' to guess. I don't think it matters whether it would have had impact. I worked in the election unit at NBC News in

1982. There was a rule then. It wasn't a law, but it was a rule, an ethical standard. A state would not be called until the polls were closed. What's happened to those ethical standards?

FRANKOVIC. The rule has actually been somewhat different. The rule has been that a state is called when all the polls are closed, or in the states that have multiple poll closing times, when the vast majority of the polls are closed. This has been the practice for decades. It was a practice in Florida in 1998, when we called Jeb Bush at 7 P.M.; and in 1988, when we called George Bush at 7 P.M. We called Bill Clinton in 1996. We called Ronald Reagan in two elections. Now, all the news organizations who've conducted their reviews have recommended that this change. They are recommending that a state not be called until all the polls are closed there. That doesn't just mean Florida. It also means states like Kansas or Michigan, where 1 percent of the polls are in a different time zone. The rule that's been in effect since the 1980s—and Congress was aware of it—all the networks have now said that will change.

ELIHU KATZ (University of Pennsylvania). I think we ought to say something about the ceremony called election night. It's a combination of a show and a ceremony of reconciliation. I would say it's a move from contest to reconciliation with the announcement of the results and the concession and so on. It's very educational. People begin to understand how the system works. They also used to see that it's fair. Now the question is how did this deteriorate? The answer is that it deteriorated because first of all, it's misrepresented as a race. God knows who won, but the race is over. The networks are presenting it as if it's a real race, but the race is only how fast you can open the ballots, one, and two it's how good the statisticians are. This is a totally different show and it's part of the entertainment, but it has a serious impact. So these different things have to be balanced. There's something good about it, but it's deteriorated into a kind of corruption.

FRANKOVIC. The people I work with are all overwhelmingly serious individuals who take what they do very seriously. The process that we used and the presentation of it is something that news organizations have been doing for a long time. Saying who has won is a statement about an event that's already happened. It happens in the states as they close. We have been aware for a very long time that a lot of people are distressed about the fact that the U.S. election system involves multiple states that set their own rules about elections even during a national election. Polls can close as early as 6 P.M. Eastern time or as late as midnight Eastern time. What's happened in the last twenty years, ever since the 1980 election, when Ronald Reagan was projected the winner at 8:15 P.M. by NBC (not by CBS until 10:00 at night, after Jimmy Carter conceded) is that this election system of multiple states and state rules has created concerns about the impact of what happens in the East on people in the West. It has also resulted in changing the way a lot of people vote. Oregon is entirely vote by mail. There is very little opportunity for Oregon voters to be affected on election day by what's reported at 7 or 8 or 9 o'clock at night. Half of the votes in Washington State are cast absentee. In California, 30 percent are cast absentee. Other states have large numbers of absentee voters. People are changing the way they vote. In the election of 1964 and the big Johnson win, when the call was made without exit polls, based only on vote totals from sample precincts, the same things were said. Since 1964, at least, CBS News has proposed and supported uniform poll closing. That bill passed the House in the mid-1980s and it is likely to pass the House again this year. That means that a national election with one set of candidates on the ballot is going to have a uniform poll closing. It will be uniform nationwide. Who knows what else the Task Force on Elections is going to do in terms of recommending federal government support for better election systems.

JAMIESON. In the transition, I would like to ask a question of the Republican representatives who are here. Is the Republican theory about what happened as the result of the first Florida call that the Bush vote was deterred, or that the Nader vote was encouraged to shift to Gore, or is it some combination of that? It appears that the theory is that there was a depression of Bush vote, rather than that the Nader vote would shift to Gore as a result of the perception that the election was close.

ROVE. I would say nobody goes to sit in the stands and eat the popcorn and watch the game when somebody's already called the game over. It's understandable.

FRANKOVIC. There actually has been a lot of research conducted over the years since the mid-1960s, and it is interesting, because at least one of those pieces of research—which I have some problems with, because it relies on recall in January of what you did in November—suggested that the impact was greater on supporters of the winner than on supporters of the losers. That would mean that in California, in the West Coast in 1980, it was Reagan voters who stayed home and not Carter voters.

ROVE. I can't quote you an academic study, but I can tell you that ten minutes after Florida was called, the chairman of our campaign in California was on the phone to me. "We're coming apart," he said. "I'm getting reports from all of our phone banks all across the state that people are getting up and walking out." An hour later, he called me saying "I'm getting reports of people in the Central Valley and in Orange County having people walk into the polls and say they've called it, it's over, and people getting out of line and going home." Now, I don't know if there's a scientific way to prove that, but I do know that when you get the anecdotal evidence of people literally shutting down phone banks two hours before the polls close because everybody is getting up and walking out saying it's over, that this had real impact and we ought to treat it with respect as having a real impact and understand its consequences.

FRANKOVIC. I hope that you do not think that I am treating this with anything less than the respect that it deserves. This is something that I take very seriously.

ROVE. I understand that, but to say that simply we've called elections before and since this is done by professionals seems to me to beg the fundamental question: should you be doing this in the first place?

FRANKOVIC. That is why we and all the other news organizations have proposed uniform poll closing, and said that we will now not call in a state while any polls are open.

ROVE. Maybe the answer is to say that states should not release the results of federal races until a uniform release time because the networks are in the entertainment business, not the news gathering business when it comes to election nights.

GANS. The uniform poll closings would not have corrected any of the major errors of this election. Al Gore was called in New Mexico after the polls closed, George Bush was called in Florida after the polls closed, Maria Cantwell was called in Washington after the polls closed, George Bush in the Washington primary after the polls closed. The networks do not have the right to purvey inaccuracy and influence the result, and they're doing all of those things by not reporting the actual results.

FRANKOVIC. We are humiliated when we are wrong, and uniform poll closing would have meant only that we would be wrong, and that we would be humiliated. Nobody would be charging us with affecting the outcome. They couldn't.

GANS. That doesn't deal with Karl's point about California.

FRANKOVIC. But uniform poll closing nationwide . . .

ROVE. But it's impractical. How do you have uniform poll closing when you have four time zones, five if you include Alaska?

FRANKOVIC. The bill is in the House. Congressmen Billy Tauzin, Ed Markey, and John Dingell are cosponsoring it. It passed the House in 1985.

Five

Mark McKinnon

Mark McKinnon was the director of media for the Bush campaign in 2000. He also held that position on Governor Bush's reelection campaign in Texas in 1998. He has for many years been a media consultant to Democratic candidates and corporate clients. He has also advised campaigns in Africa and South America.

I'm not going to try to run through the strategic framework of the campaign, but rather just focus on the media and try to give you a little bit of behind the scenes rationale for what we were doing and why we were doing it and what we thought might have worked and what didn't. I'm also, for time purposes, going to skip beyond the primaries and go right to the general election.

When you looked at this race on paper, we had a lot of tough hills to climb. First of all, you had the economy, and just given the historical perspective on the economy that was a huge hill for us to climb. But also, when you looked at the issue matrix on this election, all the issues that people cared about were typically Democratic issues: education, Social Security, health care. So, we knew that while we probably couldn't win on those issues, we had to at least keep them close. Fortunately we had a candidate who had been talking about those issues, not just in this campaign but for years as governor in Texas. So there was a platform there, and a history. Our strategy was to stay close on those issues. Those were issues that Bob Dole had been wiped out on by 20 or more points. We also tried to address the personal attributes: shares your values, ready to handle the job, truthful, and strong leader. As Fred pointed out earlier, the two attributes where we really held a substantial lead were on "truthful" and "strong leader." A lot of what we were trying to do was neutralize those issues that were important and reinforce those attributes.

It had never been done before, but we looked into it and realized that there was no reason that you couldn't spend RNC dollars after the convention. Historically, they had always been spent before the convention. We came to a conclusion that those dollars, or at least the bulk of those dollars, would be better spent after the convention. And I would argue that when you look at presidential races, the conventions almost wipe out anything before them, and it's almost like the races start over again. We did some advertising to make sure that we didn't get overwhelmed, but we held a large portion of that money back, which I think was strategically a good decision.

So we started our paid media campaign at the convention. The problem we were facing was how, in a terrific economy, do we argue for change? That was an ongoing internal conversation and challenge we were facing throughout the campaign. How do you argue for change when people are so satisfied with the conditions that they're living in? One way was to acknowledge the good times. We realized that it would be swimming up river to try and suggest in any fashion that the economy wasn't in good shape. So what we did was to say that because things are good, now's the time to do hard things. Now's the time to make tough decisions and you need a strong leader to do that. So we started off with a series of three commercials that communicated that particular message.

Announcer: A lot of new Americans arrived today. They were

Mark McKinnon. Photo by Kyle Cassidy.

neither Republican nor Democrat, but someone held them close and hoped they'd be healthy, learn a lot. It takes leadership to give everyone a shot at the American dream to make sure every child learns to read, to strengthen Social Security, to keep America strong, to unite, not divide, and let every American look at the White House and be proud. George W. Bush for President.

Announcer: Once in a hundred years our nation has this chance to be at peace, to be prosperous, to do something good with it all. This is the time to tackle the tough things. Shouldn't our grandkids find Social Security secure? Shouldn't we raise standards so every child learns to read? Shouldn't we keep America strong and rebuild our military? Shouldn't the president unite, not divide and renew America's purpose? George W. Bush for President.

George W. Bush: This is the moment in history when we have the chance to focus on tough problems. It's not always popular to say our children can't read, or Social Security needs improving, that we have a budget surplus and a deficit in values. But those are the right things to say. And the right way to make America better for everyone is to be bold and decisive, to unite instead of divide. Now is the time to do the hard things.

The next ad is a little bit of a stab at alternative media. This was the first political dot-com ad; it was more of an experiment than anything. We did it when we launched our website. We did it in a couple of target markets to see if it would help drive people to the website, and it did. It doubled the number of our hits in the localities where it ran.

After the convention we got our convention bounce that we'd hoped for. One of the things I argued all the time about the campaign is that there are three events the campaigns control in the general election: the selection of the Vice President, the convention and the convention speech, and the debates. Those are significant moments in every general election campaign where numbers can move substantially. We had hoped to do well on all three of those, but we realized that winning any one of them could provide an advantage in the long run. So, one of the things we were also trying to do was to push the message that Governor Bush was ready for the job, and the convention speech helped do that. We got great feedback from the convention speech. He looked presidential. So we put up some spots cut out from the convention speech. Here again the idea was to push that Bush was a strong leader and ready to handle the job.

George W. Bush: Seven of ten fourth graders in our highest poverty schools cannot read a simple children's book. Millions are trapped in schools where violence is common and learning is rare.

Announcer: The Bush education agenda—reform Head Start, focus on reading, restore local control, triple funding for character education, hold schools accountable for results.
George W. Bush: Now is the time to teach all our children to read and renew the promise of America's public schools.

George W. Bush: We will strengthen Social Security and Medicare for the greatest generation and for generations to come. I believe great decisions are made with care, made with conviction. We will make prescription drugs available and affordable for every senior who needs them. You earned your benefits. You made your plans. And President George W. Bush will keep the promise of Social Security, no changes, no reductions, no way.

The second of those spots was partly defensive in nature because the Gore campaign was going strong into Florida now, heavy with the health care message, and we saw pretty quickly that they were moving fast and hard, and that we had to get there quickly. I think in retrospect I'd rather not have done a second convention spot. I think we got the juice out of the first one. This was a period where Gore was getting his legs. So we were trying to cover Florida. There was also a lot of internal debate about getting quickly to a contrast message. We got seduced by the numbers and the convention, and suddenly, Vice President Gore had a terrific convention and a great selection in Lieberman, and the race was dead even. So we wanted to make clear that there was a contrast, and a real difference in the candidates, so we put up a contrast message on HMOs to counter what was going on in Florida on school accountability and on taxes. I love how this whole tax debate has come around. There were a number of times during the campaign where President Bush got a lot of pressure to back off his tax plan, and it's a testament to who he is and his kind of leadership that he stuck to it despite that pressure. Now he ends up, like good leaders do, in the right place at the right time on the right issue. But what's interesting about the tax issue is that, while from a public perspective it may not have been a particularly up-side issue driving votes at the time, we discovered that Gore's targeted tax cut was a real negative for him. When you talk about targeted tax cuts to people, everybody thinks it's somebody besides me. So we decided we'd hang that around his neck and put up this contrast message.

Announcer: Al Gore's prescription plan forces seniors into a government run HMO. Governor Bush gives seniors a choice. Gore says he's for school accountability, but requires no real testing. Governor Bush requires tests and holds schools accountable for results. Gore's targeted tax cuts leave out 50 million people, half of all taxpayers. Under Bush, every taxpayer gets a tax cut and no family pays more than a third of their income to Washington. Governor Bush has real plans that work for real people.

We're now in what we call "Black September." We're still struggling. If we're the solution, there's got to be a problem, so we're trying to figure out what the problem is. We'd always felt that education was a great platform for Governor Bush, because it had always been a priority for him. It was something that people cared about. Alex Castellanos came up with the idea of an "education recession," which was a great idea, because it touched the right buttons about that issue. People sensed that there was an education recession and that it was something we could fix, something we could address. So we did another series of education spots. And again, a lot of what you'll see in the design and the presentation of this message is that George W. Bush is a different kind of Republican, that this is not the kind of Republican that you're used to, he's reaching across old boundaries and borders, talking about issues you're not used to hearing Republicans talk about.

Woman: I have seen a big difference since he has been Governor of the state of Texas.
George W. Bush: We want every child to be able to access the greatness of America. And it starts with teaching every child to read.
Woman: He said, if you need it, we'll get it for you. We have web sites, we have grant programs and we have George leading the way. People ask me why have I followed him so intently in this education and reading. I followed him because he's been a leader.
George W. Bush: Reading is the new civil right, because if you can't read you can't access the American dream.

Announcer: Under Clinton/Gore America is in an education recession. Fifty-eight percent of fourth grade kids in our schools can't read. But Governor George W. Bush has a plan. He will require schools to be accountable for our children's learning, for higher standards. When it comes to our children's education it's not about spending more, it's about expecting more.

George W. Bush: Sometimes if you want things to be different you have to make them different.

George W. Bush: I believe we need to encourage personal responsibility so people are accountable for their actions. And I believe in government that is responsible to the people. That's the difference in philosophy between my opponent and me. He trusts government. I trust you. I trust you to invest some of your own Social Security money for higher returns. I trust local people to run their own school. In return for federal money I will insist on performance, and if schools continue to fail we will give parents different options. I trust you with some of the budget surplus. I believe one fourth of the surplus should go back to the people who pay the bills. My opponent proposes targeted tax cuts only for those he calls the right people, and that means half of all income tax payers get nothing at all. We should help people live their lives, but not run them, because when we trust individuals, when we respect local control of schools, when we empower communities, together we can ignite America's spirit and renew our purpose.

There was a lot of discussion about this spot. This was going to be the last spot, but several people—Karl Rove and Don Evans and Matthew Dowd—came to a consensus view that the debates were critical. We were down 4 or 5 points, and the time to turn the race around would be during the debates. By the last week, it'd basically be over as far as any real moving of the numbers. It would be electronic wallpaper on TV. People wouldn't be able to distinguish between ads. Doing a sixty-second spot in any campaign is always a tough sell. It's using up twice the dollars for half the message. We felt strongly that people were either going to see Governor Bush for the first time in the debates or they'd be refocusing on the race. So it was a real opportunity for us to put his best face forward, the best synthesized message and to do it in a format of sixty seconds, where it not only was, but it had the appearance of being, substantive. When people see a sixty-second spot, it just feels more substantive. And it is, because you get more information in. We also hooked on to a message that got some traction for us, which is, "I trust people, he trusts big government." We knew that was working when they put up spots pretty quickly following, saying, "not for big government." So we had them trying to defend themselves on the big-government issue. "I trust people, he trusts big government," was a simple, easy to understand explanation. It tied the Governor's talk about trusting people to invest their own Social Security money, trusting people to make decisions on Medicare, choices and local school districts. It was a neat, clean message right at the time of the debate.

We started that spot the day of the first debate and ended it the day of the third debate. That trust message ran during that entire period. This is when it helped that Gore had the problem with exaggerations during that same time frame, while we had a trust message out there. We put a lot of weight behind that spot, and finally, in the last couple of weeks, we saw we had a problem with married women. It was always a problem for us, and we'd brought it a little tighter, but they were pulling away again. So these next couple of spots were designed to reinforce and strengthen our numbers with married women.

George W. Bush: Today, our children are forced to grow up too fast. Parents need tools to help them protect and nurture their families. We need filters for online content in schools and libraries, family hours for TV programming, character education in our schools, more effective drug prevention, tough school safety so children learn discipline and love go hand in hand, and more flex time for parents. I believe parents today need allies, not adversaries, to help raise moral, responsible children.

George W. Bush: How come the hard things don't get done? Because they're hard. If we really want to make sure no child gets left behind in America we need the courage to do some tough things. We need to raise standards in our schools. We need more accountability and more discipline and we need to stop promoting failing kids to the next grade because we've given up on them. It's easy just to spend more. Let's start by expecting more.

The last spot we did for two reasons: we wanted to keep on the offense against Gore, but we also wanted to be on defense on Social Security, because they were hitting us on the Social Security message. So we used this as an opportunity to both defend and go on offense, by showing some video of Gore and his own words.

Announcer: Remember when Al Gore said his mother-in-law's prescription cost more than his dog's? His own aide said the story was made up. Now Al Gore is bending the truth again. The press calls Gore's Social Security attacks nonsense. Governor Bush sets aside 2.4 trillion to strengthen Social Security and pay all benefits.

Al Gore: There has never been a time in this campaign when I have said something that I know to be untrue. There's never been a time when I've said something untrue.

Announcer: Really?

Six

Lionel Sosa

Lionel Sosa was a media consultant for President George W. Bush in the 2000 campaign. Since 1980, he has been a media consultant in five presidential campaigns. Since 1995, he has headed the largest independent Hispanic advertising agency in the southwest, Garcia LKS, which was founded by his wife, Kathy Sosa. In 1980, Mr. Sosa founded Sosa, Bromley, Aguilar and Associates, now Bromley Communications, the largest Hispanic advertising agency in the U.S. with billings totaling over $150 million. He is the author of a book entitled The Americano Dream: How Latinos Can Achieve Success in Business and in Life, *published by Dutton. He is currently a fellow at the Institute of Politics at Harvard's Kennedy School for Government.*

Why was there such interest in the Hispanic vote in 2000? And why were both presidential candidates speaking Spanish for the first time ever? The answer is quite simple. Hispanic voting power is huge. There are more Hispanics in the United States than there are Canadians in Canada, about 35 million. If you were to take the U.S. Hispanic population and consider it a Latin American country, it would be the fourth largest. And it would be the richest. Period. Hispanics are becoming more involved in the political process, more educated, and more aware of their power.

It is a voter group that's becoming so large that the Democrats can no longer take the group for granted and the Republicans can no longer ignore it. In the past, this happened a lot. Twenty years ago, 85 to 90 percent of all Hispanics voted the straight Democratic ticket. Today, it's very different. George W. Bush proved that in Texas in '98 when he got 49 percent of the typically Democratic Hispanic vote. This vote will not remain in the Democrats' column in the future. It is a vote that Republicans can attract consistently by doing the right things, and that is inviting them, involving them, and connecting with them.

I was first introduced to Ronald Reagan in 1979, when we were hired to do his Hispanic media. I introduced myself and told him, "I'm on your team to help you get the Hispanic vote." He smiled, put his hand on my shoulder, and said, "Well, that's going to be easy."

At the time, 85 percent of all Hispanics voted Democrat. I was stunned at his optimism, and asked, "Why do you think it'll be so easy?"

He replied, "Hispanics are Republicans. They just don't know it."

"Tell me more," I said.

"Well," the governor continued, "look at the conservative values of the Hispanic. Hispanics believe in the same things we believe in: family, hard work, personal responsibility, and good moral values, faith in God."

That one-minute conversation set in motion the communication strategy for the work I have been doing in political advertising for twenty years. If we bond our convictions and our beliefs with Latino conservative values, it will make little difference to the voter whether you are a Democrat or a Republican. If you deliver a strong, consistent message with emotion; if you really put the proper resources behind it—not putting it on the back burner, or toward the end of the campaign, asking "What are we doing

Lionel Sosa. Photo by Kyle Cassidy.

about the Hispanic vote? Well, let's take some of the commercials we've done and translate them." It doesn't work that way any more than it would work if you took Spanish commercials and translated them into English hoping they'd do the job in Iowa.

Our strategy for getting the Hispanic vote is simple. First, be out there in an important way. Make sure that Hispanics know you need them. Make sure you have enough messages out there so that they feel that they're important. Ask them for the vote. TV and radio commercials should be in English as well as in Spanish.

Number two, connect emotionally with the values of family, hard work, personal responsibility, opportunity. Talk to our desire—the Republicans' desire, the candidate's desire—of leveling the playing field. All of those are things that Hispanics will respond to. But don't try to convert them into becoming Republican. That doesn't work. It's the candidate, not the party. Emphasize those attributes that Mark talked about, attributes like "cares about me," "is truthful," "is a strong leader." If you do all of these things, all issues can be handled, because a voter understands that a candidate with strong qualities like these will be able to handle any issue that relates to them.

Hispanics don't respond well to commercials that have the candidate pontificating to someone off-camera. This is like making a speech to someone else, not to the viewer. They like eyeball-to-eyeball communication. To Hispanics, and maybe to every other voter, that little box called a television set is nothing more than the communications medium that should do what you would do in person. I think you saw that in many of our commercials. There was a sense that "George W. Bush is talking to me." Even if there are five or six people watching the TV at the same time, each individual perceives the message as being directed only to him or her. That's extremely important. Also, not putting the candidate in a big presidential setting, where he's more important than the voter. Instead, the candidate should be depicted in a living room setting, or some other casual setting, using body language that says "We're friends. We understand each other." When all is said and done, so much of connecting has to do with: Does he like me? Do I like him? Do I trust him? Is he a good, strong leader? For Hispanics, the issues having to do with education, Social Security, and health care can be best delivered after the candidate has connected on a personal level.

We produced thirteen spots for the 2000 campaign in both English and Spanish, and also an Hispanic video for the convention. The effort worked. Bush got 38 percent of the Hispanic vote nationwide. Lance Tarrance just completed a national poll of Hispanic voters. He asked questions like "Do you feel more important in this campaign? Do you feel that one candidate or the other was talking to you? Did it feel different this year? Did you feel that your vote made a difference?" When all those questions were asked, Hispanics replied, "Yes. I felt more important this year. I did make a difference, and I can make a difference in the future."

The first two spots you will see feature George P. Bush, the "third most eligible bachelor in America" according to *People* magazine. I first saw him when he and I were in San Bernardino, California, to be surrogates for the governor. We were told, "This is a group of important Democrats, and we need to get our message out." What I didn't realize was that these voters were not just ordinary Democrats. They were Cesar Chavez United Farm Worker Union Democrats! As I arrived, a fellow making a speech at the podium declared, "The enemy is amongst us."

"This is not going to be easy," I thought.

Then George P. Bush arrived. It was the first time I'd seen him in about twelve years. When he was twelve years old or so, he was part of a commercial I produced for the elder Bush. When "P" made his way into the room, and he was introduced, the Latin Democrats didn't ask "What are you doing here? You're a Republican." Instead, they came to him. The crowd got bigger and bigger. And he hadn't even been introduced! But word was getting around that George P. Bush was in the room. One man about forty years old came up to him and said, "I want to shake the hand of the man who will be the first Hispanic president of this country."

"This kid's got something," I thought. "We need to have him do some commercials." That was a natural thing, because he is part of the Bush family. A Latino is part of the Bush family! To Hispanics in the United States, "family helping family" is the best thing anyone can possibly do. All of the commercials you will see now were produced in English and in Spanish.

George P. Bush: Why vote for George W. Bush? Because he believes in family, because he supports education, because he knows we all are the new face of America, because he wants no child to be left behind, because it's time for a change, because he understands our culture. (*Speaks in Spanish*) Because he's a great guy. (*Speaks in Spanish*) This is the reason. (*Speaks in Spanish*) why I'll vote for him, how about you? How about you? (*Spanish*). How about you?

These bilingual commercials were very effective. Now here's a look at the five-minute video that played during the convention.

Woman: The first time I saw George W. Bush in person was when he was marching down Guadeloupe Street at the Mexican Independence Day parade. He was smiling, shaking hands. He was walking, not riding in the car. The day was hot. He was sweating, but he loved it. Kind of reminds me of the days when the Kennedys used to go to the Latino neighborhoods, to our neighborhoods. They loved everybody and everybody loved them. That's how I feel about George W. Bush.

George W. Bush: I've been asked many times what makes up the character of a man. I think it's a lot of things, where you grow up and how, the values you're taught, the friends you pick, how you see family and how you see others. When you grow up in Texas you have a certain vantage point. I made a lot of good Latino friends back in Midland. I don't forget them. Where I come from, cultural diversity isn't just something you read about, it is something you see every day. It's part of your life. It's the people you know. In my case it's family.

George P. Bush: I'm a young Latino in the U.S. and very proud of my blood line. In many ways, I'm like any other American. I believe in opportunity, a level playing field for everyone and the achievement of the American dream. I have an uncle that is running for president because he believes in the same thing, opportunity for every American, for every Latino. His name, the same as mine, George Bush.

George W. Bush: I'm proud of the Latino blood that flows in the Bush family. As a consequence I've learned about the culture, a bit about the language and a lot about the Latino character. I've learned that my values and Latino values are the same, conservative values.

Man: It didn't matter to him whether you had a lot of money or you didn't have any money or that you were Latino or black or whatever, he's the same person. That made you comfortable around him.

Man: It's comforting to know that quite possibly George Bush could be president of this country and we can have someone that can understand us, someone that's not pretending or needs an adviser to understand the Hispanics in Midland and Texas. He can actually say, "Hey, I know what they mean."

George W. Bush: Latinos enrich our country with faith in God, a strong ethic of work and community and responsibility. We can all learn from the strength, solidarity and values of Latinos. Latinos come to the U.S. to seek the same dreams that inspired millions of others. They want a better life for their children. Family values do not stop at the Rio Grande River. When you really get down to it, we're all immigrants. This country continually reinvents itself with new generations of immigrants and each generation enriches America. The opportunity to achieve the American dream, that's what it's all about. But when you talk about the American dream and opportunity, it implies a level playing field for everyone, and it isn't always that way. Latinos and African Americans, many times, get the short end of the stick. Sometimes the discrimination is obvious, other times it's so subtle, you could miss it if you're not watching. But my friends tell me this, if you're on the receiving end of it, you feel it.

Man: You know, he was the first governor that actually stood up and said, we will not have immigration bashing in the state of Texas.

Man: There's not a better man that I know for President. And I'm going to back that up by voting for him.

George W. Bush: Latinos contribute so much. And in return they deserve a full promise of American life with reforms that say to Latinos, this is your country, this is your home.

Man: George, just be yourself, Buddy. Go get 'em.

BRUCE BUCHANAN (University of Texas). What do you think about the vote share you got this time from Hispanics and what are your plans for the future?

SOSA. Our goal was 35 percent. In his first race as governor, George W. Bush got 24 percent of the Hispanic vote in Texas. Once the Hispanics got to know him he got 49 percent of the vote four years later. In this campaign the *L.A. Times* reported that he got 38 percent of the Hispanic vote. If that doubles, that's 76 percent of the vote for next time—*that* won't happen. But it is possible that the 49 percent he got in Texas can be transferable nationwide in the next election if everything goes right. Remember, only 10 percent of all Hispanics saw these ads. They ran mostly in Florida and in New Mexico. So the big states like Texas, California, and New York had no media. Even so, with only 10 percent of the voting population exposed to this message, it made a difference. In the end, Bush got 1 1/2 million more Hispanic votes than Dole got four years ago; 850,000 more votes than Clinton/Gore got four years ago; and 6,500 more Latino votes in Florida than Gore did. Without the Latino vote in Florida, Bush would have surely lost the state, and thus the presidency. All with no recounts.

RUTH MANDEL (Rutgers University). When you look at women's voting patterns, we're always talking about assumptions about monolithic voting behavior and monolithic attitudes. I'm wondering, when you describe the Latino vote in your description of the community and the outreach and in the advertisements, it sounds as if there's an assumption that a pretty similar message is going to appeal across all the different groups, and yet when we talk about the Latino populations, we're always taught to make separations according to Mexican Americans, Cuban Americans, and so forth. But is there enough commonality that you're assuming there is something called a Latino vote in this country?

SOSA. Absolutely. If you were to take that example into the general market, you would ask, "Are New Yorkers the same as Texans? Is a California surfer the same as a Wisconsin dairy farmer or the Louisiana Cajun?" You would conclude no, they're all different. The same message couldn't possibly apply. Well, that's overdissecting it, but it's usually what a lot of folks do in the Hispanic market. They just assume that because we come from different countries, we're totally different. The real truth is that we've got more similarities than we've got differences, and that's what our agency focuses on. It's the similarity of values, of opportunities, and being American heroes, not helpless minorities in need of government aid.

Seven

Bill Knapp

Bill Knapp has helped to develop communications strategy for such leading Democrats as former Senate Majority Leader George Mitchell, Senators Robert Byrd and Jay Rockefeller, Adam Clayton Powell, and Attorneys General Mike Moore and Skip Humphrey. In 1996, along with former partner Bob Squier, Knapp was the leader of the Clinton/Gore and DNC creative teams and oversaw the creation, production, and placement of more than $100 million in advertising for this effort. More recently, Knapp served as a senior adviser to the Gore/Lieberman presidential campaign as a member of the advertising and communications strategy team. Responsible for overseeing the production and media placement of all television and radio advertising, he played a major role in the writing and development of all campaign spots.

There were four main legs to our advertising strategy. One was to raise questions about the Texas record. It was very, very important to us. There was a cycle in this campaign, more than in the past in my view, in which people—the press and the public to some degree—would fall in love with someone, learn to dislike him, and then look for someone else to fall in love with. There was a period early on where they were in love with George Bush, before McCain scuffed him up. Early on in our issue ads, it was important to continue to tell people about the Bush record, to raise questions and doubts about him based on that record, and to make sure he couldn't regain that bubble that he had early on, that enthusiasm for him. So that was very, very important for us. Our strategy in busting the bubble was to raise questions about his readiness. Fundamentally, what the Texas record was about was, is this guy ready to be president. It was not an explicit question we were going to raise early on. It was more implicit early on. It became more explicit toward the end of campaign, but we wanted to provide the information, the infrastructure, to say it another way, so that we could make the argument later on. We wanted to create character doubts as well. And their campaign was relentless in creating character doubts about us. Our character doubts were a little different, only because the research dictated that. Theirs was more by its nature, ad hominem and more at Gore personally, with regard to the lying and not getting things straight. Ours was more about whom he represents, who he fights for, and the values he has from a public policy perspective. Trust me: we tested the other. We tested ad hominem attacks against him. They were not effective. We tested spots about the draft. We tested spot after spot where we showed his screw-ups and his inability to communicate smoothly and effectively. We used that technique in '96 against Dole very effectively, but we could not get ads that worked well in 2000 against Bush for that.

The other thing we knew we needed to do was introduce Al Gore. We couldn't really do that in the primary period because the audience was too small, our budget was too small, and we didn't have the big national stage for March 7, to unveil more about Al Gore as the process went along, because we were taken over by the coverage of the Republican primaries. I'm not complaining about that. It worked to our advantage. We were happy about that, but we knew that we needed to introduce Al Gore. We also knew that we couldn't do it with issue ads. I would have preferred a campaign where we introduced Al Gore, where we told them more about him and then we moved more aggressively on the Bush record. But because of legal restrictions as to what the DNC can say and do, the bio ad, which was a cornerstone for us, could not run until after the convention. So we had to delay the introduction of Al Gore. In a weird way, the public could not have their "fall in love with Al Gore" stage until very late in the election process, which is something we were unhappy about, but we really didn't see a way out of that box.

The two other advertising strategies were obviously to draw contrast on key issues. The Bush campaign was very, very effective at taking the sting out of some of those contrasts. It was a constant frustration to us that you would make progress on education. Bush spoke about education from the heart, it seemed sincere, it seemed real. That was a problem for us. Those ads in general tested well. We did not have a good attack line on education. We could not find a good vulnerability to rip down his education positioning based on his Texas record. I'd love for you guys to share with me some of his vulnerabilities so I can use them in another campaign. But we really couldn't find an effective way to blunt his education offensive. Which, in a weird way, was a sort of reverse wedge issue. It was an issue that went to our wedge, to our constituency, and we had trouble beating it back, and that was a frustration. I think we ran, in the end, one thirty-second education ad. Stan Greenberg desperately wanted others. He was a constant voice for our need to do this. I think we had the wherewithal to be more effective, finally, toward the end, where we figured out a way to do it, but we had to get to the other things as well, and defend ourselves on Social Security and win the prescription drug fight, so we couldn't get to it. Education worked very effectively for the Bush campaign. We ultimately wanted to

Bill Knapp. Photo by Kyle Cassidy.

raise fundamental issues of his readiness, so we pushed hard on the issues, but we also pushed hard on that Social Security ad you saw at the end to raise the fundamental question of whether he was in fact ready.

There's nothing groundbreaking about the tactics. We were relentless in targeting the key swing states. We didn't vary from that. Initially we had some hope for Florida. We thought it could work for us, but we were skeptical about it. At first, it was two thirds we wanted to keep it alive, and one third we wanted the Republicans to waste money there. The choice of Lieberman changed that dynamic a little bit for us. I don't think we fully understood how dramatically it did at first, and Florida became very real to us. During the entire course of the campaign we spent a lot of time and effort to develop a system to incorporate our state polling into our targeting model, and to adjust the buy by media market, not by state, as we rolled along, with the key variable of adjusting for price. Stations kept jacking up the cost of the issue ads, and as a result the lowest unit rate went up, so the rates for the candidate ads also went up dramatically. That was a dynamic that didn't exist in '96 that we had to take account for, the constant changing of prices. That affected, pretty dramatically, how much we would spend in particular markets to make sure we were being as efficient as possible. We spent a lot of time on that.

Unlike '96, in 2000 we had a different way of testing ads. In '96 we did mall tests. In 2000 we did focus groups. The sixty-second ad that Mark McKinnon showed tested really well in the focus groups. We had constant problems with that. The notebook ad that Alex Castellanos did was a real pain in the neck. It took us a couple of tries to get the response to that down right. Obviously, we did a pretty aggressive job of airing state-specific media where appropriate. In our tracking of electoral votes, at the end we saw ourselves with 181, Bush with 209, and 147 up for grabs. In between the leaning Democratic states and the strong Republican states is where we focused our media. Some states would fall in and out, but in general the toss-up states were the focus. We spent our money pretty much in the same states as the Republicans did.

We spent about $10 million in the primaries. Prior to the party convention, Gore spent nothing. The DNC spent $28 million. The Bush campaign spent, by our recollection, about $3.1 million. The RNC spent about $21 million. After the conventions, the Gore campaign spent about $45 million; the DNC $31 million, for a total of $76 million. Bush by our recollection spent about $63 million, almost $20 million more out of the Bush campaign itself than the Gore campaign spent. The RNC spent about, by our recollection, $59 million. So that's $122 million to $76 million from the conventions to the end, an important and sizable difference. You can subtract California where they spent some money and we spent none. We spent in Ohio and ended up pulling out of Ohio. So the campaigns do waste a little bit of money. You end up spending money in places where, in retrospect, you wish you hadn't. But that is a substantial financial difference.

I think the Republicans decided that in '96 they got outspent, and were not going to allow it to happen again in 2000. They didn't. That was a key decision they made. They focused on the fund raising. They were more than competitive. They blew us away.

A couple of comparisons. Florida: total Gore/DNC $11 million, total Bush/RNC $21 million. Now I don't know that much about paid media, but I know that $10 million is worth 537 votes. In Michigan, total spending was $13 million for us, roughly $15 million for them, a $2 million difference. Missouri, 8.5 to 9.7. Oregon, 5.9 to 7.3. Pennsylvania, 14.7 to 18.9. West Virginia, 830,000 to 2,095,000. The difference makes me really unhappy. It's interesting being present at the creation in '96 and in 2000 and I just want to share with you briefly some of the differences that I saw.

I don't agree with Matthew's characterization of the '96 ad campaign. Although there is some disagreement even among Democrats I thought the preconvention DNC ad campaign was effective because it reinforced events that were happening.

Gingrich seemed too radical, too far to the right, and the Republican Congress clearly was not able to manage the responsibilities they were entrusted with. I think the ad campaign helped reinforce those perceptions. In 2000, events constantly and consistently conflicted with our paid media. The reality of the campaign versus the reality of the news media created a discordance that was a problem for us, and occasionally for the Bush campaign as well. It was a close, hotly contested campaign. There was an incredible echo chamber early on. A study found that 80 percent of the press coverage of Gore was negative. An inordinate amount of it was negative and process oriented. The *Washington Post*, for example, had a constant filter on. It was always about Gore and Clinton, Gore and Clinton, Gore and Clinton. You got your fiftieth call from Ceci Connelly wanting to do the seventieth story on the relationship between Gore and Clinton and, frankly, I think we managed it badly. In other words, that was the reality of this thing in hindsight: our job was to manage it better. I don't think we did. There's also the mindset of the "big story." The news cycle has become increasingly vicious. You don't just have the networks now, you have CNN, Fox, Chris Matthews. So there's a whole bunch of reasons why it's gotten more competitive.

I want to spend a moment on what I call Poll Nation. I'm not a pollster. I don't pretend to be one. The daily tracking polls reported in the press floated all over the place. They did this in '96, by the way. Once in '96 there was a 19-point swing in one day, and they tried to explain the swing on the air. On the one hand, I do find it funny, but having lived through that in '96, they still did it in 2000, and they did it with a vengeance.

One of the things coming out of this election that does need to be looked at is that if you spend the time polling the right way, if you spend the money to poll the right way, if you're patient to poll the right way, you can get the right numbers. Stan had the right numbers. I'm sure the Bush campaign had the right numbers. The networks, the news outlets don't have the right numbers. And they need to step back and figure out what they're going to do about it, or they'll continue to pervert the system.

I just want to make another point about the reporting. On September 11, Gallup had Gore 49, Bush 42. That's a seven-point spread as I count it. It was reported as Bush/Gore deadlock. Go to October 8: Gore 41, Bush 49, eight-point lead for Bush. Headline: Bush Maintains Solid Lead Over Gore. October 28: Gore 42, Bush 49, seven-point lead. Same as the September 11 lead, except reversed. Bush is reported as having a solid advantage. We have a five-point lead on September 17. That's a "narrow lead." My point here is, the analysis is totally at variance with reality. I'm not picking on CNN . . . Well, maybe I am. I'm picking them on purpose. But the point here is, you can see this in poll after poll and outlet after outlet.

In 2000 we had an inability to demonize the opposition, and I credit the opposition for this. The Republicans contained themselves. They followed his lead. They didn't make any major mistakes in governing that we could capitalize on. Bush did a really good job of moderating himself rhetorically. That made it very hard for us to demonize him. Education, in our mind, played a central and critical role in that. We tried to figure out the sharpest, harshest way to characterize what we thought were his real positions, to take his statements and try to confront people with them, but people weren't accepting it. It was very frustrating. It was a funny mix with voters. They understood the prosperity, they liked it, they credited Clinton with it some, they credited Gore with it not at all, but there was a sense that it's something they could take for granted, that it was bigger than government, it didn't have much to do with government, so it was very hard to focus their vote on the issue of prosperity. Obviously, the money played a very important role. As we got down the stretch, what we could spend, and the Republicans' ability to have two tracks of media on earlier, to have them heavier, put us in a bind in terms of the number of spots we could put out and how we could deal with their attacks, but also stay on the offensive.

Their move to the center clearly worked well. We lost an opportunity. After New Hampshire, we went on a little bit of a bender on campaign finance, we lost an opportunity to stake out some very critical positions on taxes, on crime. I find that April, May, June period probably one of our worst internal campaign mistakes. Education was very effective for them. Social Security for us was very effective. It was not about privatization. I must have tested a dozen ads trying to get at the privatization thing, to try to get at the big picture: his Social Security plan versus our plan. They would not work. It was a funny thing in focus groups. Men loved the investments because they were going to be as rich as Donald Trump. Women said, "My husband's going to invest the money, I don't know." So there was a little bit of that, but not enough for us to drive a truck through. In the end, the dual promise was the thing that we found most effective, because it dove-tailed with our broader argument of "Is he ready? Does it add up? Do you know everything you need to know about this guy and his ideas and what he wants to do?" It didn't please young people that he was making a double promise. It didn't please older people that he was making a double promise.

The clarity and consistency in their attack on ethics and the anti-D.C. rhetoric was very, very effective. They did not vary from that very much. My hat's off to them on that. It proved to be, in many ways, determinant. Our questions about the Texas record were also effective. I am curious that there were only two instances where the Republicans actually responded to ads that we did. They responded once on the environment—we couldn't believe they did that, because we would have loved a $100 million argument on the environment. We had a little bit of a dust up in Michigan, which worked to our advantage on the environment, over "Earth in the Balance." Then they responded to the Social Security ad, and we responded with the former Social Security administrator making the case that Bush's plan was no good, and in fact promised a trillion to both sides. But they chose never to respond to those attacks. I'm curious about that.

I'm also curious about compassionate conservatism. To us it was effective as a reassurance that he was a different kind of Republican. In our own polling, in our own focus groups, in our own thinking, it seemed to fail with African American and Hispanic voters. There was a little bit of anger in the end, particularly among African Americans, that he seemed to be saying one thing, but the reality seemed a little different. It may be that if they got Hispanic and African American votes based on compassionate conservatism, that was icing on the cake. But the strategy was really not to hemorrhage with moderate women, where a Republican can very often hemorrhage, but where we can work a wedge in, and get votes. In that way it was very effective.

Their tax plan, by our minds, failed. It didn't test well. But ultimately, the Bush campaign did stigmatize our tax cut as too narrow and too small. We paid a price because of that, and it left an opening for them to make us seem more liberal. We had a heck of a time trying to demonize Bush.

The strategic petroleum reserve has been talked about before. This is the final thought that I want to leave you with. It's a pigeon-head analysis I want to share with you. It doesn't take a rocket scientist to know that values are going to be an important part of the campaign. In 1996, values were central to Clinton's campaign. In fact, a lot of the values language that you now see in the campaign was appropriated in '98 in the midterm election, and used effectively by the Bush people in 2000. So I'm taking credit for the Bush victory.

Bill Bradley and George Bush had weirdly similar rhetorical views about prosperity: it's great, but it's not enough. Bradley kept saying it's not how high the Dow is, it's how good your heart is. Bush had a similar take on it. I do think there's a tension in people—they know they're doing better, but this value stuff pulls at them and tears at their hearts a little bit. They don't like the values direction of the country. This is not an indictment of Clinton. If you see it in terms of freedom and prohibition, we're in more of a prohibition era than we are in a freedom era. People are concerned about these things.

The Vice President, because of who he is and the job title he has, could not claim credit for the prosperity. It was a constant frustration for us. We tested 17 trillion ads to try to get the prosperity to work effectively as a positive for us. It was an extremely difficult thing to do. If it was easy, trust me, we would have done it. If it was hard we would have done it. We found it impossible to do, which is not to say it didn't ultimately work for us. But Stan made the point that it was our closing argument, not our opening argument. We had to achieve a lot before it could be effective. We had a situation where it was hard for the Vice President to gain in prosperity, and the Bush campaign was taking the values to personal side of the Vice President and trying to shred him. They did a very good job of attacking him personally on ethics, raising value-related questions. We couldn't take credit for the prosperity, they were going after us on the value-related dynamic, and the combination was very tough on us. Obviously it wasn't so tough—we won the popular vote, it was virtually a tie. But the dynamic was very difficult for us to break out of.

THOMAS MANN (Brookings Institution). This is a question for both parties. Could you give us a sense of the extent to which you were constrained in any way by the part of your media budget that was being financed with soft money for theoretically issue-advocacy ads? That is, what is the nature of the link between your campaign budget and the party-coordinated spending, and the soft money-financed issue ads?

KNAPP. There are a host of very specific differences in terms of what you can say and what you can do. For example, there was not an effective bio that we could run using issue ad dollars—and we didn't have hard dollars to do it with—prior to our convention. So the sixty-second positive bio ad did not run until after we became the actual nominee. I remember that there was a feeding frenzy as we were preparing to go on with the first issue ad. The national press was obsessed with "it's going to be a bio ad right? It's going to be a bio ad. It's going to be a bio ad." I don't know where the rumors were coming from, but we could never run a bio ad that was effective with soft money.

So that's an example of one restriction in the issue ads in terms of what we could say, and the timing of when we could say it.

MANN. I'd like to hear from Mark McKinnon on this. Obviously Republicans outspent Democrats because they were able to raise this additional money. Is that right?

KNAPP. Well, they spent almost $18 million more by our count out of the campaign committee itself.

MARK MCKINNON (Bush campaign). That was an allocation issue. They spent dollars, too. They just spent them elsewhere.

MATTHEW DOWD (Bush campaign). I agree with Bill. There are some restrictions, but if your question is, did we feel we had to do something with one that we really couldn't do with the other—other than the bio ad, and then you obviously couldn't, there had to be separate film, etc.—but you pay for the issue ads with RNC money, and then you do the rest with your campaign. In our case, the RNC ads carried more of the negative and the comparative, and the Bush ads carried more of the positive message.

KATHLEEN HALL JAMIESON (University of Pennsylvania). Let me ask for a clarification. Could you not under the law use soft money, if you put the bio ad together and at the end said "So call Al Gore and thank him for having such a loving relationship with Tipper," if you avoid elect-or-defeat language?

KNAPP. You might be able to, but our lawyers weren't comfortable with that.

JAMIESON. But didn't the Dole bio ad run as issue advocacy in '96?

KNAPP. It did. Yes, it did.

JAMIESON. Nobody sent anybody to jail. There's a lot of confusion.

KNAPP. Well, there isn't just confusion among scholars. There's confusion among consultants.

MCKINNON. I think that they are well meaning, but these distinctions and differences are completely blurred. Because the laws are so unclear, Bill was doing both DNC and candidate ads. We had Alex Castellanos doing it, but the reality is we were talking to Alex about it, and so the laws don't seem to make much sense. They need to be fixed. But as they currently stand, nobody understands them. Everybody does what they want, and it's murky and confused.

DOWD. It seems to put lawyers in charge of making political decisions in a campaign situation. To some degree, that hinders clean communication. It doesn't necessarily help. We're all pretty sure it's not having the impact it was intended to have.

DORIS GRABER (University of Illinois, Chicago). You've told us about a lot of successes and a lot of failures. Is there any message in this in terms of what works and what doesn't work? Why was it that you couldn't demonize George Bush? Was it just the particular circumstances, or is there something wrong with the advertising? Was it a misjudgment of some kind? Is there a general pattern judging from this and previous elections, in particular this election, about what works and what doesn't work?

KNAPP. With hindsight at 100 percent, there are a million things you could do differently. But the most important lesson to me, from both 1996 and 2000, is that it is important in a national campaign to grab the center and effectively hold it, and to control the debate around it. Both campaigns struggled with that, perhaps us a little more than them. The other thing is that values politics is here to stay awhile. Stan raised some very intriguing questions as to why it's here. It's too narrow to say it's Bill Clinton. There are some bigger things at stake—the cultural wars. Effectively using the values issues, as I learned in '96, can be very effective. I learned in 2000 it can be very effective. I learned it one way in '96 and another in 2000. I think we were more effective in '96 than in 2000 for a host of reasons.

Broadly speaking, I would say that sometimes there is a tendency to focus on issues, and say we're going to win this issue fight, we're going to win that issue fight. Sometimes you do lose the forest for the trees a little bit. We are in an era of personality politics and values politics. I think you saw it emerge pretty strongly in '96, and it's stronger in 2000, and exactly how it's going to play out in '04 and in the midterm in 2002, I don't know.

MONTAGUE KERN (Rutgers University). You spoke about April and May when the campaign really, from your view, should have focused more on taxes and campaign finance. Why did it not do that given what you had learned earlier about the role of values?

KNAPP. It was a difficult period. We had this horrible financial bind where we could not advertise. We were out of money except for the ability to move Air Force Two and do some of the basic things that a campaign could do. We were in a total media blackout. So some of the malaise that occurred was just situational. In other words, we didn't have the wherewithal to do it. We didn't have the resources to communicate. We had maybe $45 to $50 million, and the Bush people had $100 million. We didn't have as much money, so there was a limit to what we could do.

We were slow in making the transition in mindset to a general election campaign. We stayed focused on Bradley, probably through March 7 and March 14, more than we needed to. We listened to the Washington echo chamber a little more than we should have. I take partial responsibility for that. That was a mistake on our part. It's very difficult to run a campaign and not get yanked around sometimes by the echo chamber and the conventional wisdom. For example, I've always thought Forbes made a huge mistake taking his foot off George Bush's neck and not staying negative in the primary. I think he got bludgeoned into it by a press corps that kept asking "why are you being so negative?" Sometimes you pay a little more attention to that than you should. I think we lost sight of the ball a little bit.

JAMIESON. Let me ask the last question just for clarification. I thought I heard the Republican consultants say that they did answer the Social Security attack on a trillion dollars promised to two groups and I hear the Democrats saying they didn't.

KNAPP. Well, there were two that they responded to. Social Security was one, and the environment was the other. The Social Security one we responded to right away.

JAMIESON. Do you see their ad that quotes the Gore statement about the dog and the family member, and then shows Gore basically saying "I never lie"—do you not see that as another response to Social Security?

KNAPP. No. My view of that ad is that it backfired badly, and it almost cost them the election. I thought it was a great ad, and when I saw it I cringed. But they ran a specific Social Security response ad with Bush saying he's not going to mess around with Social Security, and we did a response to that. The ad was a really good ad. I think it was not a bad way to end, but given the drunk driving revelation, it was potentially very dangerous. While people thought it was a long time ago, there was a little uneasiness that they hadn't come out with it earlier. The truth is, he hadn't been straight, and he was running an ad saying Al Gore's not straight. People aren't stupid. So that ad created some problems. It wasn't on long enough to remain a problem, or be a big enough problem.

JAMIESON. Could we just get a quick response from the Republicans to make sure we got the chronology right? Did you view that as a response in some way on Social Security? And did you see it as a backlash ad?

MCKINNON. That is an interesting perspective. We did it both as a response and to keep a little bit of a boot heel on Gore. But everybody's got their own analysis about what happened in the final days of the campaign, and that's a new one, and an interesting one, and one I hadn't thought of. But I think it's a relevant observation.

DOWD. On the Texas record, which this is related to, and on whether this ad was a response ad, we made our own attacks on ourselves about seven months before election day: an attack on our Texas environmental record, an attack on education, an attack that we caught ourselves attacking us. We put various responses to those ads, to figure out what we thought was a vulnerability. Actually, we thought the Texas record was THE vulnerability. In '92, Clinton didn't run on his Arkansas record. Clinton ran on change.

Our whole argument was, "here's what we did with Texas," and if that was blown up, that was a problem. But the problem we confronted responding to it was, we couldn't just say "Oh, by the way, that's not right. Here's all the stats," because when we researched it we found it didn't move the ball back very far. The only way we could really respond to those ads was an attack on Al Gore's truthfulness, that "this guy will say and do anything."

So any time you saw that trust stuff, it was trying to deal with the Texas record without getting in the weeds on the Texas record, because if we did, it was a loser for us.

MCKINNON. Our sense from focus groups is that people would play back to us the vulnerabilities. People are now pretty sophisticated to the extent that if there's an attack ad, and there's no response, they will say "It must be true." They're looking for the counter. You didn't want to have that extended fight.

Eight

Alex Castellanos

Alex Castellanos, principal in the media-consulting firm National Media Incorporated, has served as media consultant to five U.S. presidential campaigns. He has helped elect or reelect nine U.S. senators and six governors, and enjoys over two decades of political consulting experience both in the United States and abroad. Castellanos, a native of Havana, Cuba, is fluent in Spanish and English. A Moorehead and National Merit Scholar at the University of North Carolina, he lectures frequently internationally and in the United States.

Thank you for the opportunity to be here with you today. I always learn a lot at these events. I've learned today that we lost, which was news to me.

I feel a little bit like we're watching that Japanese soldier who's hanging around in the cave for forty years after World War II.

It's not over till he says it's over, but I've been on the other side when things don't work out the way you'd like and I hope we all remember that this is something that we're all privileged to be passionate about and to care about a great deal and that you do invest a lot of yourself in it. So I'm not going to begrudge anyone clinging to victory as long as possible, especially those who work in paid media. I just wanted to help put things in perspective. I was looking at how much America spends on advertising for things other than politics. There was an article the other day that said about $500 million was spent on the Republican side, including issue ads.

The campaign itself, on the Republican side, spent a couple of hundred million on advertising. I assume something comparable was spent on the Democratic side.

Just as point of comparison, the Walt Disney Company in 1998, the last year for which I have numbers, spent $1.3 billion. Pepsi Cola spent $1.2 billion. McDonald's spent a billion. L'Oreal spent $800 million, but then, they're worth it. Anheuser Busch, god bless them, only spent $630 million. And I did my part to support them. The Bayer people spent $600 million, which is more than was spent on issue advocacy last year. Mattel spent almost as much as politics, $529 million. Dog food, $461 billion. Each of the top 100 advertisers individually spent more than the Republican effort for president this year. Government consumes about 38 percent of the gross domestic product in this country; people work until sometime in May to pay for it all, and you're spending less than L'Oreal choosing the course it will take. Perhaps the amount of money spent on politics is not the problem. Maybe it's how much is spent on government.

It's good to see Rick Berke of the *New York Times* here. He fixed my low profile problem this year. I sent him a Christmas card. I have to see if he got it. Down at the bottom I wrote on it a little note, "Rocking around the Christmas tree," and I capitalized the R and the A, and I didn't hear anything back, so . . . Subliminal messages we had there.

We can talk about that if anyone is interested. I feel like I was caught riding the unicorn there, doing what does not exist. You know there is no such thing as subliminal advertising in America. There is a tremendous fear of it going back to the old book from the fifties, *The Hidden Persuaders*. This came along at the time of

Alex Castellanos. Photo by Kyle Cassidy.

the Red Menace and was all part of the fear of Americans being manipulated by evil advertisers. I know it turned into a great TV story.

I regret that I put folks I care about and work for and fight for in a situation that consumed a hunk of the campaign. But it sure did. Shortly afterward, I was sitting in a meeting when the phone rang. It was John Harwood of the *Wall Street Journal*, who said, "Alex, I hear you've been fired by the RNC." I said, "Well, I don't know. Maybe you could ask them." I handed the phone to Maria Cino who was at the other end of the table at the meeting and said, "Maria, John Harwood would like to talk to you. I think he's ruined your surprise."

One of the things that made a huge difference is that we had a very cohesive team. You learn a lot about folks when the wind blows and the storm comes. You learn who sticks with you and who doesn't. Those who do are the kind of folks you want to work for.

I ran across an interesting piece of research the other day from the guy who did the work on Folger's coffee. He does this weird, avant-garde research you can probably charge a lot for. He wanted to learn how to sell more Folger's coffee, what drives it. He found the key concept relating to coffee was mother. Mom. You develop these associations when you're young. Your mother makes coffee. You get up in the morning, there's your mom in the kitchen and she was making the coffee. So that's why, in the Folger's commercial, the young kid comes home from the war, cranks up the coffee, his mom smells it and comes down the steps and . . . That's one of the things that built the brand, Folger's. What do you associate with the president? What are the drivers? He said it was a real easy call. He said, "It's entertainment."

The point he was making was that your president is in a lot of ways Johnny Carson. He's the head of the national political household. He comes into your home and tells you how things are doing. To a great degree, whoever can do that job is the guy that America wants to elect.

This is not just about a list of issues and keeping score. It's a little bit bigger job than that, especially when you're living in an age of communications when your president's going to be in a box in your living room or your bedroom all the time. Having worked for candidates people don't like, I like to work for this kind a lot better. This is a really neat idea, that you can work for candidates people like; I highly recommend it. But it's not just a question of likability.

Bill Clinton changed what being a Democrat was. It used to be that a Democrat was just health care, the environment, the "mommy bear" side of the equation. Then along came Bill Clinton, saying, "It's the economy, stupid." All of a sudden Democrats were talking about tax cuts, and eventually even welfare reform and school uniforms. He changed what a Democrat was.

Something really powerful has happened now, this time on our side. We've seen the first New Republican. There was a time the Republican Party was this dark force, very dark and pessimistic and anticommunist and anti-this and anti-that. Along came Ronald Reagan, and all of a sudden it got a little more optimistic, and there were tax cuts and progress and hope.

This time, we went beyond even that. This time, there was a fellow who, by his very nature and personality, said, "Hey, not only are we going to talk about moral values, and right and wrong, and not only are we talking about tax cuts, but I care. I like people. I want to help." He got a chance to do things on education and Social Security. I think one reason he was so hard for the Democrats to demonize was the simple fact that he's not a demon. That made a big difference. The challenge for us now as Republicans is going to be to institutionalize what comes so naturally and is such a great and wonderful gift for this one individual. The genius of this campaign was being able to bottle this.

This is the first campaign like this for us. How do you know it was a good campaign? Because you're going to see it again. This is going to be a model for Republican success for a long time to come.

I couldn't agree more that Clinton was the vulture in the tree, overshadowing the whole election. How you could have embraced him from a distance, or if there was a way for you to win on that one, I don't know, because he was such a powerful force. One of the things Clinton did was spend eight years teaching America that every day the president is going to ask them how he's doing and do they love him. America got hooked on him that way.

Clinton, in a way, was the last of the "me generation" of politics, a very selfish politics. That's why Gore's misstatements were relevant. The misstatements were a generational thing as well. He was drifting back into a selfish politics, a little more juvenile, less mature politics, where it's all about me and my success and political expediency. That's what those misstatements did. But the Yuppies, the dominant political force, are growing up, and getting older. One of the things we saw was maturation, that America likes grown-ups now. Maybe we're all getting a little older, so there is an appreciation for people like Dick Cheney, who talks about politics and not just about himself.

That's why the campaign was able to display George Bush as a different kind of Republican. He did it, personally and culturally. I'd love to find ways for me to take credit for any of it, but it is just who the gentleman is.

Another challenge on the other side of the aisle was that to go across the middle of American politics requires a certain sense of optimism. I think Reagan has proven that, I think Clinton has proven that. And populism is pessimism. It is very hard to do it in a bright sunshiny, less angry way. That was a particularly difficult situation. Now we're left with the challenge of bipartisanship.

Friends who do a lot of writing in Hollywood tell me that the way you write movies is that the good guy and the bad guy always come in conflict over the same thing. No conflict, no movie. They always fight over the same thing.

The days when Republicans had the economy, welfare, and

crime and Democrats had Social Security, health care, and the environment are gone now. Now we're fighting to see what works, who can help the most people. We have Al Gore doing that fatherhood ad, trying to go across the spectrum to the right, being the daddy bear, the head of the political household, and Bush talking about education. We're going to meet in the middle and fight about a lot of these things. If this is anything like a Hollywood movie, for the next few years there's going to be plenty of opportunity to have vicious partisan fights over who is the most bipartisan. With the advantage of the presidential pulpit, a president with the right demeanor can win that fight.

Something ought to be done about calling these elections before they're over. Someone made the point that when they call these states, they are just covering something that has already happened. Well, not in a federal election you're not. There's no point in going to the game when you know it's over. That kept a lot of folks at home. Just because you have the power to do something doesn't necessarily mean it's the right thing to do.

We shouldn't have to pass a law and put a gun to their heads to make the news media do the right thing. What's the old *National Lampoon* cover? Buy this magazine or we'll shoot this dog? The news media shouldn't require others to put a gun to their own heads to make themselves do the right thing.

I thought this was actually a fairly positive campaign. Please don't tell anyone. It could put me out of business. There was a lot of positive messaging coming out of both the RNC and the Bush campaign, laying out an agenda. For a Republican to draw even on Social Security and education not only scores points on those issues, but says he's not going to screw you on other things, like the environment. President Bush is that kind of guy. Also, that little Social Security card in the TV commercial you just saw was a piece of stock art we found. Right before getting ready to put the commercial on the air, we noticed the name on the card: Bob

Jones. It just happened to be there on the piece of stock art, so we had to fix that. A lot of that was designed with Gore's attacks in mind. Getting that information out early was a preemptive strike.

I always felt that every day George Bush was on camera, life was getting better. Every day that Al Gore was on camera, life was also getting better for us. There was a fifty-minute focus group at the Republican convention where George Bush stood before America and talked and things just went great. There was a tremendous opportunity for him to look America in the eye and be exactly who he is.

On the environmental ad, our strategy was just to deflect the attack and not really go after Gore on the environment, but to make it a hypocrisy message. In fact, we changed the tag on the original ad. It said originally that Gore was wrong on the environment. We said no, that's not the message. "Gore is Clinton" was the message.

The point is that the days when a Bill Clinton can't talk about welfare or tax cuts for the middle class and the Republicans can't talk about education are over.

The point on those last two ads is that because of Gore's convention speech, because of Gore's populism, he gave us an opportunity to push Gore left of Clinton, and we certainly tried to do that. The original version of that ad, which tested pretty well, was: This is Bill Clinton, new Democrat. Give him credit. The economy has done pretty well under him. Al Gore is proposing three times . . . In other words, even if you like Clinton, he's here, and Gore's over there to the left. That's what that messaging helped accomplish. The message at the end of the spot is that Gore threatens prosperity, that a Gore administration would not be the Clinton administration, so even if you like the economic prosperity, Gore is not only divorced from it, he threatens it. That brought the whole package together.

KARLYN CAMPBELL (University of Minnesota). I'm perfectly

convinced that Al Gore came across as unlikeable, but what kind of data do you have about the likeability of George Bush? I sure heard a lot of stuff about smirking, arrogance, that kind of thing from my students. Do you have data about that?

CASTELLANOS. I know that any time you put him on camera talking to folks, looking them dead in the eye, even when they thought he smirked a little bit, at the end of the day, the question was is this a good guy or someone who is going to put his own political success first? No. That selfishness never registered.

BILL KNAPP (Gore campaign). My take on it was that from our perspective, the smirk was a big problem for him. At least on our side of the divide, the sense was that you recognized that, and that's why his major non-smirk coming out was his convention speech. At first I thought he had a catheter, because I thought he was peeing in his pants for the first twenty minutes, but the truth is, it looked to me like he had been coached mightily to not smirk on that speech. So it was clearly something that from our perspective was a problem. It was a constant playback in focus groups, especially for women. They didn't like it, and the Bush campaign managed to get rid of it. When he was doing better and we were doing worse, it was less of an issue. When we were doing better and he was not doing well, they didn't like it. By the way, just for the record, I don't share your characterization of Gore with the voters.

CASTELLANOS. I don't think we ever found the so-called smirk to be a problem in any of our focus group research. We always thought that we were in pretty good shape regarding perceptions of each candidate as a person. We always found Bush to be likeable and genuine. What we ran into more was the contrasting truthfulness of the two candidates and people's lack of trust in Gore. They perceived him as pandering to people and exaggerating. In terms of personal flaws, that was far and away more important and more a factor in the election than whether people liked Bush's smile or not. We always thought Bush's personality was an asset in the campaign.

DANA GOLDTHWAITE (Annenberg School). I noticed you fast-forwarded through one of the ads that showed how Gore claimed he invented the Internet, which became a huge source of late-night jokes, especially toward the end of the campaign. I'd like to ask someone from the Gore campaign why that wasn't dealt with by the other side. It was initially said that the way it was phrased, and the spin on it, might have been inaccurate. Why wasn't Gore's real connection to the Internet, or what this exaggeration was about, ever explained?

KNAPP. My recollection is that that was a dust-up that happened early. We felt that it was taken out of its proper context, and had a life beyond the facts. In one of the debates with Bradley, Gore even tried to explain it as a mistake in how he spoke, but we felt strongly that the more we tried to talk about it, and tried to explain what we thought in many cases were manufactured misstatements and exaggerations of human mistakes, the worse it became, and that we couldn't relitigate things from the distant past while the Republicans were stirring up new ones. We really didn't figure out a way to address it directly.

CASTELLANOS. Any time Gore stepped on one of those land mines, the test was, was he Clinton? It brought back all the character issues. Not only that, it made him smaller. He was Clinton junior, not even a very good Clinton. Part of the Gore mission was to emerge from the shadow of the president and become his own man. Every time there was one of those character misstatements, he became not only Clintonesque, but smaller, and that was a big problem.

DAVID BIRDSELL (Baruch College). I have a different kind of Internet question. You showed a spot a while ago in which you used television to drive people to the Internet. You said that was successful at the time. You said you aired that in two markets, I believe. How did the Web fit into your strategy overall? The general book on the Web this year is that except in isolated fund-raising areas, it was pretty disappointing as a political tool. What did you want it to do for you? What did it do for you? And what might you expect it to do for you in the future?

KARL ROVE (Bush campaign). We found that there were more cost-effective ways to achieve what we wanted to do there, which was to expand the number of people on our Web list. In the campaign, we used the Web for a wide variety of purposes. We had identified 400,000 people as Bush supporters and activists. We used the Web to communicate with them and to generate activity. It was a very active recruitment avenue for us. It helped us recruit literally tens of thousands of volunteers. We could send out an "e-blast," as we called them, to people in a certain state, and generate a lot of people that we didn't otherwise know were coming.

We became so convinced that this was useful that toward the end of the campaign, we worked with our very active IT group, which included John Chambers of Cisco and Bob Herbold of Microsoft. Michael Dell chaired our group. They were on the telephone for a conference call every two weeks. These guys had a combined net worth probably larger than many countries in Africa, and they were actively involved in the campaign. Toward the end of the campaign, they energized a six-week effort called "E-Champions," funded through the Republican National Committee, which was an attempt to generate a series of activities, including sending them material to register all their family members, sending them volunteer materials, sending them things they could send to their own email list. In six weeks, we generated—from a standing start—1.1 million new email addresses.

We had a combined e-mail address list of close to 1.6 million Republicans. The "E-Champions" was self-funded by Silicon Valley types who thought it would work. Then we stumbled into sending an email message asking them for money. It funded the effort all over again. It was enormously successful. In fact, we've maintained it to this day. The number of new volunteers who showed up in our headquarters because somebody sent them email was just extraordinary.

BRUCE BUCHANAN (University of Texas). Obviously you won, at least by some definitions. Nevertheless it's also true that you aspired to do better than you did in terms of the absolute numbers. In the spirit of self-analysis that some of the Democrats displayed, what would you do differently?

CASTELLANOS. I have the impression, largely from the reaction to the vice presidential debates, that the American people liked the vice presidential candidates. They weren't as scarred as the presidential candidates. I wonder if that's true. It might not be. It might have a lot to do with the news media's overpackaging, overmanufacturing.

KNAPP. I don't buy the premise. I think there was a little bit of reporting about that, but I didn't see that in any of the numbers we saw. The vice presidential debate was a very critical moment. The aftermath of the first debate set up this peculiar dynamic in that second vice presidential debate. We knew Cheney was going to be good, but prior to that debate, Cheney was definitely a drag on the ticket. We were getting more coverage in spot markets than he was.

That debate totally flipped that around for him. It's not that it destroyed Lieberman at all, but it really helped Cheney, and very importantly, provided an alibi for people being for a less experienced candidate. They now knew that Cheney had a lot of experience.

It was a critical moment in a perverse but interesting way. Since it was so nauseatingly positive, it set up that peculiar second presidential debate. In the end, that didn't serve us well. It didn't draw any of the important contrasts we had intended, and was so contrary to the first presidential debate in tone and feel. In a weird way, it set the preconditions to the second debate and was hurtful in that regard. But while there was no unbelievable love affair with either of the candidates, neither was there any massive disenchantment with either of them.

CASTELLANOS. I think Bill is right. People felt warmly, but not deeply, toward both of these candidates. After all, it was a surface biography. Cheney was vaguely remembered as the successful commander of the defense department during the 100-hour war. Lieberman came across as a deeply religious person who felt comfortable in his religion. These were for different reasons, and both were positive and comfortable. But people, while they felt positive about both candidates, did not feel deeply about either vice presidential candidate.

I also think Bill is absolutely right about that debate. To me, Cheney won due to an unscripted response to a clearly scripted moment: as part of the class warfare argument, Lieberman made a joke about how wealthy Cheney was. Cheney has a wicked sense of humor in private, but the American people hadn't seen it. This was their only moment to do so, and he came across with not one, but two very good lines. As a result, he won the debate, but what got me was that somebody had clearly planted in Lieberman's mind to come out there and take a whack at this guy. To say that he was a rich guy and had made a lot of money. That was the populist mindset of the Gore/Lieberman campaign at that point. But it set up the second debate.

We tracked the comparative impact of presidential visits, vice presidential visits, and advertising on the ballot. It was interesting to watch the Lieberman impact. In the aftermath of the convention, it almost rivaled that of Bush and Gore, but it fell rapidly. Cheney rose slightly, but after the vice presidential debate and before the second debate, Cheney passed Lieberman in impact in a market where he visited. So if Cheney went to a market, he had a bigger impact than if Lieberman went to a market. That continued until the end of the election. Now it wasn't a big effect, but it was a significant change and I trace it to that moment in the debate. Before that, it was like fighting one against two. After that debate, it was two on two. That meant a lot.

KATHLEEN HALL JAMIESON (University of Pennsylvania). Not to offend you, or encroach on your creativity or minimize your effectiveness, but there is some sentiment among those who have tried to reform politics in a benign fashion that maybe the process would be well served if we could find a way to get candidates and their consultants to voluntarily agree that, just as a norm in politics, when an ad goes up, the documentation will go up on the candidate's Web site, so the reporters can find it, the people who are interested in it can find it, and there is some sense of accountability built in for people who would like one further step of information. Is there any problem that you would see with that?

ROVE. We did that. Nobody cares.

CASTELLANOS. Most of the time, you have to do that when you put up an ad, whether you put it on the Web site or get it out in the press kit. That's filtering down from presidential to every level. We have to keep the academics fed. It's very important to provide them with ads to dissect.

JAMIESON. This isn't a question about what you did in the past campaign. I think both campaigns behaved admirably in this campaign in terms of providing information to people who needed it. The question is, if you wanted to simply make this a norm in politics, so that it would happen in gubernatorial races, as people increasingly put Web pages up . . . Do you see a way to easily institutionalize it? Do you see any problems in institutionalizing it?

CASTELLANOS. I think it's happening.

ROVE. It doesn't matter. We put our donors up on a daily basis, with a searchable engine on our Web page. Every day we got the money in, we put it up on the Web page so you could see whom we were getting money from. We scored no points at all. The same with the media backup. If we put the backup up for our ads on the Web page, who cared?

JAMIESON. What would you have liked to see that would have made you feel better about having done it? Would you like to see editorials saying, that was a good thing, Karl? Would you like an academic award? Would you like to see lots of hits? What is the reward structure? I appreciate that you did it, but when you don't feel rewarded, how does one ensure that you're going to do it in the next election, or in any other campaign you ever run?

ROVE. This doesn't fit the paradigm of the people who run television stations and print newspapers. They could care less about this. They want a different kind of focus and a different kind of answer and they're not going to offer an alternative answer. It's like campaign finance reform. We want openness, but if you're open, no one cares if you put it up on the Web page so we can figure it out. What we want is *our* answer of openness, not *your* answer of openness. I'm all for it. We ought to continue to do it so at least we can sleep better at night, but in terms of expecting anything great out of the media, who arguably are the principal commentators on the process, it's not going to happen

JAMIESON. If we were to ask the consultants who ran the presidential campaigns this year to issue a statement with us saying that we think it's a good idea to do this, we don't expect any rewards for it, that's the way the world works, but we think it's a good idea to do it and we're going to do it in the future, do you think we'd get corroboration?

ROVE. Lip service.

JAMIESON. Do you anticipate that when you run the next campaign you'll do it again?

ROVE. Sure. It makes us feel good and lets us sleep better at night, but in terms of being a fundamental reform of the system, I don't see it.

JAMIESON. If we could get people to use it, we'd have a small improvement at no cost.

ROVE. But here's the fundamental problem. Even if you put out backup for what you have, whether it's a Bill Knapp ad or a Mark McKinnon ad, the media are intent upon finding something wrong with your ad. They're obligated to. They're going to say, "Oh, average voter. Don't be misled by this cynical ad. There's something fundamentally flawed in it. They left out the comma." The label remains whether or not the substance endures.

CASTELLANOS. I know it's fun to watch the media guys, and we sure do enjoy the attention. But since the Bronco ran out of gas, and we don't have OJ to kick around anymore, there's a need to feed the media beast. It seems to me it's gotten a little out of control. The MSNBCs, all these guys, look for anything they can pick at and tear apart. This year you had the most positive, most issue-filled election ever, and I'm supposed to be the negative guy, right? Well, I couldn't begin to fill my day with a small hunk of the negative assault on the process and credibility and authenticity of candidates and their motives that is put out there by TV. It's a constant barrage of "let's see how these guys are trying to screw you today." All for ratings and bucks. That's fine, but then to be pilloried by the same people for doing an issue contrast ad does gall you a little bit.

JAMIESON. Let me phrase the same question to Bill. Did you see any problem with expecting candidates to document ads online?

KNAPP. No, I don't think people in campaigns will really feel an obligation to do it unless there's a voter reward in it. I will say that if you went up with an ad and didn't have documentation on the website, and the ad box said there was no documentation provided, then that could theoretically be used—by people as unscrupulous as Alex—against someone, saying their use of an attack ad has no documentation. So there is a way to recycle some of the criticism. If the press decides there's a norm, that it should be on there and it's not, and they note it's not on there, that notation could potentially be recycled in a competitive back and forth campaign. For us personally, of course there's no downside. But you pick and choose the documentation that proves your point. As a matter of course we provide documentation. As a matter of course, in most Senate and gubernatorial races I do. It satiates the elite, and they look at the website a little bit. By the way, we did a test in the Gore campaign of some banner ads. They were remarkably ineffective. We used it, basically, as elite communication and grassroots stimulation as opposed to advertising. Maybe some day it'll be more effective as an advertising medium. It's not for us now.

JAMIESON. One last point on the petitions. There appears to be a pattern in state and local races in which the reporter finds out what is incorrect because the reporter is doing an ad watch, but then doesn't document so the public can cross check, if the public wanted to examine the ad watch and the source of the ad watching. That's the concern. There's an increasing trend for consultants to hand documentation out to reporters. If we could just take the next step, even if it didn't affect a lot of people and even if there's no reward, it doesn't appear to cost anything in addition. For those who care about it, at least it helps understand how you got to the inference that you're offering in the ad. Sometimes we academics draw the wrong inference about how you got to where you were, sometimes unfairly, because we haven't had access to the same things that you are providing for reporters.

CASTELLANOS. Look at the sources of information you have today: the Internet, ten different cable news networks . . . For three bucks, you can buy a magazine that has more information than your forefathers could get in an entire lifetime. I would just say work harder, because it's out there. There's a ton of information.

JAMIESON. Alex, I promise you the next time I'm critiquing your ads I'm going to work harder.

Nine

Karl Rove

Karl Rove served as chief strategist for George W. Bush's presidential campaign. He has been actively involved in national politics since the 1970s, when he was chairman of the College Republicans. His association with the Bush family dates back to 1980, when he worked on George H. W. Bush's first presidential campaign. Over the last two decades he has been a consultant on numerous campaigns from his base in Texas. He is currently a senior White House adviser.

Now that the campaign is behind us, I can readily and finally admit that three of the four biggest mistakes of the campaign are my personal responsibility. It is true, I am the individual who said, "Yes, let's go spend two million dollars in Arizona in the primary. We can beat Steve Forbes there."

I'm the guy who said in August '99, "Don't worry about all those days that John McCain is spending in New Hampshire. Nobody is paying any attention right now."

And of course, I'm the genius of the campaign who, in early September, said, "Yes, let's by all means challenge Gore to early debates, starting with *Meet the Press*. The media will hold him responsible for his earlier statements on the issue." The fact that I still was around on November 7 is real proof that George W. Bush is a compassionate conservative. Fourth, I want to admit, frankly and freely and openly that the success of the Bush campaign is due to one reason and that is that the campaign was essentially run by Democrats.

Mark McKinnon and Matthew Dowd are former Democrats. Matthew voted in the Republican primary last year for the first time, and did not dissolve into a blob of gelatinous material. Mark worked on a Republican campaign in '98 and found the experience liberating. So the real truth is that we were able to befuddle Democrats because at the core of our campaign were two Democrats.

Over the course of the campaign, I kept a diary. From it, I have written some very important rules for those of you who are planning to be involved in a presidential campaign. I take this occasion to pass them on to you. First of all, beware of the kissing grandma in Iowa. I'm confident she will be around in four years. She will mysteriously show up at every single event, wearing that weird hat and placard and demanding to be kissed by the candidates. So beware.

Second: If your candidate runs in both Iowa and New Hampshire, remember this important piece of information. In Iowa, pork is the other white meat. But in New Hampshire, lobster is the other white meat.

Third, media polls, especially CNN's, are right at least twice during the campaign. And for your candidate, this is the most important rule of all—well, second most important rule of all: hope to, but don't try to lower the expectations. Think about that for a minute.

Now, you want to win? Four words. Earth tones, subliminable, and strategery.

I was the chief strategerist of the campaign.

Let me close by addressing two serious items. First of all, this

Karl Rove. Photo by Kyle Cassidy.

election involved an astonishing event for modern American presidential politics, and that is that George W. Bush won with a swing of 11.3 million votes. That is to say, 11.3 million more Americans voted for the Republican ticket in the year 2000 than had voted for the Republican ticket four years earlier. That's a pretty astonishing swing. With it came some pretty dramatic changes. The number of new Hispanic voters who voted for the Republican presidential ticket grew from '96 to 2000 by 1.5 million. We got more new Hispanic votes than Ronald Reagan received in his 1984 reelection, when he won the record high 44 percent of the Latino vote. Second, we won a number of states we should not have won. Not only did we win the home states of the President and the Vice President, but also states such as West Virginia, where a Republican last won an open race for the presidency in 1928. It took nominating a Catholic in that election to get those Democrats in the hills and hollers of West Virginia to vote for a Republican.

But there are a number of changes in the election that show that there is some significant political change, or potential political change, going on beneath the surface. It may not be the dramatic realignment of past elections, but both major parties' past agendas are essentially exhausted. Both parties are attempting to find new agendas, new issues, and new methods of talking about those issues to make themselves relevant.

The final thing I want to say is that I've been involved in a lot of campaigns, but I've never been involved in a campaign like this before and will never be involved in another campaign, except maybe one, like this again. Most campaigns are ego-filled shark tanks, where there are thinly disguised factions maneuvering against another, bruising battles behind the scenes that are too often carried out in full view, and a lack of confidence in or by the candidate. This was an extraordinarily different campaign. Even on the worst day, it was a joy to come into the headquarters. With that, I will conclude and be happy to answer or duck any questions that you might have.

KATHLEEN FRANKOVIC (CBS News). There's a question that I've always been curious about in this campaign. Because the

1988 campaign was like the 2000 election in so many ways on the surface, did you consciously take any lessons from the then-Vice President in Bush's victory in 1988?

ROVE. No. In fact, 1988 was the last campaign we compared ourselves to. We took some lessons from 1992, a lot of them negative in nature, but 1988 was not a similar circumstance.

FRANKOVIC. Did you expect the Gore campaign to try to recreate the Bush campaign of '88?

ROVE. No. We expected the Gore campaign to do what it did, which was to try to recreate the attack-dog atmosphere of 1993 through 1997. What was interesting to us was looking at the way Gore conducted himself in past campaigns. We looked at tapes involving his Senate reelection race against Victor Ashe, the mayor of Knoxville, to do debate prep. There is a consistency to Gore's handling of himself. There was also a consistency to how his consultants handled themselves, and that gave us a sense that their campaign would be focused more on defining Bush than on defining themselves.

I had an interesting talk with Victor Ashe. He had no chance of beating Al Gore. They had eight debates, and at every one, Gore went at him hammer and tong about Victor's record, not about Gore's record. So to the degree that we drew lessons from past campaigns, we drew lessons from the performance of Gore and his consultants in past campaigns. The principal lessons were that they would attempt to make the campaign about us, and that what we needed to do would be to try and make the campaign about us as well, but make it about who Bush was rather than who they wanted Bush to be.

EDWARD CARMINES (Indiana University). One of the remarkable things about the Bush candidacy was how he was able to hold the Republican coalition together, in terms of the Christian right and the Main Street traditional Republicans, and simultaneously reach out to modern, independent voters. That's extremely difficult, and it's extremely unusual for a candidate to be able to do that. How much did Bush himself contribute to that success?

ROVE. Virtually all. The only thing the rest of us contributed was window dressing. This really started in 1993, when he began to run for governor. He adopted four big issues he wanted to talk about while running for governor: education, juvenile justice/youth crime, welfare reform, and tort reform. He began to talk about these four issues using a distinctly different vocabulary. Instead of talking about education in the normal Republican teacher-bashing terms, he talked about the need to ensure that every child learned to read. When he talked about juvenile justice, it wasn't "Let's find the little creeps and lock them up." He said "We're losing a generation. How can we show them that love and responsibility go hand in hand?"

When he talked about welfare, he didn't say, "Let's get the welfare cheats off the rolls." He said, "We're losing some of our best and brightest to dependency on government. How can we help free people to meet their greatest potential in life?" And when he talked about tort reform, it was not about big corporations. He talked about how to hold people responsible for their actions and create an environment in which entrepreneurs and risk takers can create jobs. He had a distinctly different vocabulary.

When he got ready to run for president, the question for him was, "What do I want to talk about, and how could I talk about it in a way that I want to?" Early on, it was important for us to show that he was a different kind of Republican. That largely emanated from him. Showing that he was a different kind of Republican, one who was inclusive, optimistic, and positive and had a different vocabulary, was easy because it sprang from him. But it was one of the five underpinnings of the campaign in the primary and through to the general election.

ALEX SLATER (Annenberg School). Could you tell us about your strategy toward presidential candidate Ralph Nader? Did you have a strategy to try to expand his vote?

ROVE. No. We discussed strategies about things we had the ability to affect. Nobody had the ability to affect Ralph Nader. I did receive a couple of polite phone calls from his campaign manager. There were some nuts out there who called to talk about how we could make money find its way into the Nader campaign, but essentially we had no ability to affect Nader and we had enough to say grace over. Nader was his own engine and we didn't have any of the controls. I know that the polls will not bear this out, the polls say the Nader voter would have voted for Gore, but that's because they're civically responsible individuals answering those questions, and they lie. I think that Nader energized a group of voters who otherwise would have sat on the sidelines.

KATHLEEN HALL JAMIESON (University of Pennsylvania). One of the survey questions put up by a consultant suggested that Bush had a perceived advantage on favoring a strong military defense. I'm interested in how you got him to that point in light of the fact that if I read the budgets correctly, Gore had $100 billion set aside for defense increases and Bush had $45 billion. Gore was going to spend more, and Gore served in Vietnam. Although Bush served, it wasn't in Vietnam. Granted, the Republicans are traditionally perceived as strong on defense, and you had Cheney.

ROVE. In the first speech Bush gave, on June 16, 1999, he talked about military defense. So by the time that Al Gore—I think it was in August, or maybe even September 2000—laid out the

$100 million number, Bush had talked about the issue and owned it. Gore did not. Gore's credibility on this was suspect. After all, he had been in office for eight years, and the state of America's military was clearly in disrepair. So he had little credibility to talk about it. It was overly reactive. One of the problems Gore had was that the Gore campaign didn't seem to know what its center was. Any morning, you could pick up the newspaper and figure out what the Bush message was and what we wanted it to be. It was not a secret. We wanted 105 million voters to know what the Bush strategy was. But pick up that same newspaper, and the Gore strategy was hard to define. Their thematics didn't reinforce each other, and often clashed with each other within a short enough time frame that people said, "Geez, that's different from what I heard a little while ago." My sense is that the defense issue was simply a process of consistency, showcasing it, talking about it. One of our most effective ads was a military defense ad. By the time Gore woke up to the fact that he had a problem and attempted to mitigate it, saying, "Well, I'm going to spend twice as much," we owned the issue, and he had little credibility.

THOMAS MANN (Brookings Institution). Karl, I would love to know what your thinking was in 1997 or early '98, before Monica Lewinsky entered the political lexicon. I say that because the Democratic consultants this morning asserted that had those words never entered our lexicon, this would have been a comfortable election for Al Gore. Do you agree with that? Second, were you thinking about making this run as early as '97, in January, before Monica appeared on the scene?

ROVE. If anything, it energized the Democrat base and made it virtually impossible for us to expect anything in the way of significant gains among African American voters. The whole process rallied the African American community behind Clinton in an extraordinary way. There was already an underlying value issue, which had more to do with the way things were in Washington—the tone, the acrimony, the hyperpartisanship, the sense that the presidency is essentially all about politics and not substance, that he said one thing and did another. That was there regardless. The Monica issue probably served to energize the Democrat base in a way they had not been prior to the whole incident. The impeachment process energized African Americans and "true believers" to say there was a vast right wing conspiracy that planted this woman in the White House and directed her to embarrass the President in this way.

There was already a value issue, a character issue. I don't think Bush began to think seriously about running for president until '98. He was focused on more important things.

While the polls in early '97, showing him winning the presidential election, didn't mean a lot, they were impossible to ignore completely.

The most important decision made about that early situation was for him, in November '97, to say, "I'm running for reelection. If you're concerned about whether I'm going to run for president, I don't know. You're free to factor that into your thinking as you think about my reelection campaign." That authenticity and honesty allowed us to run a strong reelection, and gave him thirteen months during which he could stay focused on being governor and running for reelection, have that exhaust 90 percent of his time, and allow the preparations for running for president to be less. For the time that he did want to devote to the presidential consideration, he wanted to devote to preparing himself on the substance side rather than on the tactical, political side everybody else expected.

ELIHU KATZ (University of Pennsylvania). We heard a lot in the morning about the findings and the methodology of survey research polling. But the overtone of the rest of the day is that somehow, focus groups have displaced polling, certainly from the point of view of the creative people and the political engineers. Is that right?

ROVE. My sense is that Democrats totally follow the focus groups. On our side, in this campaign, we used focus groups to get some qualitative sense of situations we'd want to test. In defense of our pollsters—we had two, Fred Steeper and Jan Von Lohuizen—in the history of modern presidential campaigns, no two pollsters have derived a smaller percentage of the budget than these two guys.

We did our first poll after we launched. Bush's core belief is that the function of a leader is to define a vision and to persuade people to follow it. So the idea of running a poll to test his ideas in advance strikes him as backward. So we did our first poll and then asked, like Ed Koch, "How are we doing?"

We used focus groups as a way to test TV ads and develop some qualitative questions we wanted to test quantitatively. But even then, I suspect we did less polling than almost any presidential campaign. This campaign was Fred's and Jan's loss leader.

KARLYN CAMPBELL (University of Minnesota). I want to ask a very delicate question. When the DUI came out, I had Republican supporters tell me that this was a Democratic plot to do something horrible to George Bush. Did you know about the DUI? If you knew about it, did you make a decision not to talk about it or not to admit it?

ROVE. I knew about it. There could be a great argument as to how big a mistake this was, but yes, it was a problem. It cost us Maine, where we went from being slightly ahead to 5 points behind. I've looked at the coverage in Maine. For the last six days of the campaign, it was all over the television and the front pages of every Maine newspaper. Nationally, I think it probably cost us half a point. It cost us Maine, with five electoral votes. You can make an argument that there were points where we could have talked about it. But are we going to require every candidate to talk about everything they have done all the way back to the age of eighteen months? We could argue about it, but it's a decision that I agreed with and a decision I'll defend.

DORIS GRABER (University of Illinois, Chicago). At any time during the campaign, was there any concern about Buchanan taking part of the Bush base? Was anything done in any way to try to stop that?

ROVE. We had no concern about Buchanan. Politics is not kind to minor party figures. Particularly after he bolted the Republican party, Buchanan became a marginal figure. Our view of the election was that it was going to be a very close contest. This year, those electoral models were right. We should have gotten our brains beat in. We should not have won this election. This is a time of extraordinary peace and prosperity, so we felt the end game was going to be a very close election. So we were concerned about things that would keep people from voting for the Republican ticket or the votes that Buchanan might take away, but if Buchanan hadn't been there, we would have acknowledged the fact that Howie Phillips could have taken away enough votes to switch the election.

We were concerned about things over which we had no control, but we wouldn't worry about them. There was nothing we could do to affect Pat, and he quickly became even more of a marginal figure than we had predicted, particularly at the end, when he misspent that $12 million. I knew he was going to have absolutely no impact from the time his first round of advertising went up in Boston and Birmingham. Neither state was necessarily in play. His whole strategy was to try to get votes in states that were clearly out of play for both major party candidates: Alabama for Gore and Massachusetts for us.

FRANKOVIC. In light of what you said about how the models predicted a Gore win, let me ask you this. What could the Democrats have done that might have sunk the Republicans? What didn't they do that gave you a sigh of relief?

ROVE. Well, they were stuck with Gore. They had Gore as their candidate, so we didn't deal with the variable of the candidate. If he had boldly proclaimed, "I intend to carry forward the policies of the Clinton/Gore administration that have created this enormous peace and prosperity in the world" and did it early, and was consistent about it, it might have been problematic. But he was focused on Bush, not on himself. He was focused on defining Bush, not his own agenda, and we saw several different personas. There are two badly expressed theories of the American voter. One is that the masses are asses, have very short memories, don't recall much, and don't pay much attention, so we can write a TV spot or a speech, or contrive something about a candidate and change his colors—you know, earth tones—and this will fool them. I think just the opposite. I think that particularly in a presidential race, there is a level of clarity on the part of the American voter about who the candidates are. What they heard about Al Gore, despite the peace and prosperity and the good times, was that he was not true to himself, that he really couldn't be trusted, that he was just another ordinary pol. What added to that was his varying personae: Mr. Populist, then Mr. High Tech, then Mr. Earth Tones, then the alpha male. People just said, "Who is this guy?" So despite the fact that the times were really good, the country was at peace, and they gave very high job approval ratings to the administration, he didn't capitalize on it. He may not have been in the position to do so unless he had made a decision early on.

Karl Rove and Kathleen Frankovic. Photo by Kyle Cassidy.

There was never a question about George W. Bush. He had clarity. When you heard him talk about education, even his opponents would say, "This guy cares about it. This guy really does want every child to learn to read." When he talked about compassionate conservatism and heralding the individual and reaching out neighbor to neighbor, people knew that this came from his heart. They didn't get that sense about Gore.

After we secured the nomination, we had a plan. We said, "Here's what we're going to do to lay out a comprehensive agenda, from Social Security to education reform and more. We're going to go lay out the nuclear weapons policy that says regardless of what the Russians do, we've got too many nuclear bombs, let's reduce the nuclear stock piles. We're going to do this, we're going to do that." And we were sitting there saying, "Oh, God, what is Gore going to do? How soon are we going to be on the defensive?"

Lo and behold, we began to roll out our plan and about June, all we were facing were Gore's TV ads. We were sitting there saying either we're wasting a lot of time and energy and motion by having a defined plan of activity when the opposition thinks nobody's paying attention, or something weird is going on here that is going to give us a little bit of an advantage.

BRETT MUELLER (Annenberg School). How did you feel the media's portrayal of lower expectations for Bush going into the debates affected your debate strategy overall?

ROVE. It didn't affect our strategy. It was a recognition that Gore had deliberately tried to build up his expectations. Bush had had exactly two debates before he entered the presidential contest, one against Ann Richards and one against Gary Mauro. He did well against Ann Richards in '94. He did so-so against Gary Mauro in '98. So he was not an accomplished debater, it was not his style. Gore put a lot of time and attention into it. He loves doing it, he feels he's good at it. I was a high school debater, so I know where he's coming from. I'll tell you, plenty of times, as a high school debater, I lost the audience, but won the judge. That was the problem Al Gore had. So it didn't affect our strategy. We just recognized that he had high expectations for the debate. He expected that others would both develop and follow those high expectations and have a relatively low expectation of Bush. I said earlier on, and I meant it: you can hope to, but don't try to, lower the expectations about your candidate. You just can't do it.

MUELLER. So did you formulate your strategy then as if you were almost starting from an even playing ground?

ROVE. We needed to take him seriously in a debate, we needed to work hard at it. And we did. We had Senator Judd Gregg play Al Gore and he was fabulous. He was mean, he was tough, he was nasty. We did a lot of practice debates. We did a lot of it, and it was not pleasant. It took a lot of time off the trail, but we were serious about it because we knew it would be difficult.

MARTIN SELIGMAN (University of Pennsylvania). I have a question about a hypothetical crisis in the future and how you might advise the White House to react. Let's say sometime in the next six months, an apparently disinterested group recounting the vote in Florida comes out with a fairly convincing set of data that suggests that the intention of the voters in Florida was Gore and not Bush. What's your advice going to be about how to deal with that?

ROVE. They're going to count by five standards. It's going to be something we'll have to deal with. I have no doubt that if the strict standard of the Supreme Court is applied, we will be fine. But as somebody who watched this process, this could unnerve anybody. We monitored the counts in Florida. Palm Beach drew its precincts in an entirely random order. The theory would be that as you went along, any changes would be randomly distributed. When they counted 271 precincts, 42.54 percent of the total number of precincts, Al Gore's net gain was 1. Projecting that out would guarantee you a relatively small change in the county. By the time that we got to 49.76 percent of the vote being counted in the county, 317 precincts, Al Gore had picked up a net of 26, leaving you the impression that it would be a relatively modest increase if you finished the other just over 50 percent.

When you got to 58 percent, he had gained 58 votes, giving

you 137 votes that he would likely have gained at the end. When you got to 65 percent, he had gained 72, again raising the total. When he got to 69 percent, he had gotten 94 votes, again raising the total. When he got to 77 percent of the votes, 493 of the precincts, he had gotten 115. With 500 precincts or 79 percent of it, he got to 122.

If you look at this rising trend line, there are points where it flattens out when we put observers in front of them. When Governor Pataki shows up and sits three feet away from them, suddenly they moderate. But after an hour or two, when Governor Pataki goes away, the line rises again. Now lest you think that this is an unusual experience, unique only to this county, in Broward County, when 24 percent of the vote is counted, and again, randomly drawn, Al Gore has a net pickup of 78, which projects out to a total of 324. When 50 percent is counted, he's got 143, which projects out to 286. When 69 percent is counted, he's at 188, projecting out to 272. When 82 percent is counted, he's at 230, projecting out to 278, and when 96 percent is counted, he's at 296, projecting out to 308. Miraculously, in the last three points, 81 percent of the precincts randomly drawn and counted, he moves to 348. Picks up in the last four precincts, nearly 60 votes.

Anybody who thinks this process of counting ballots was done in a deliberate, fair, and impartial fashion is kidding himself. Now, since then, these ballots have been run through the machines a couple of times. The Miami-Dade ballots were run through the machine four times before being sent to Tallahassee. Remember, these are punch cards, and these punch cards are designed to be run through the machines a limited number of times. They were run through the machines four times on the two days before they were sent to Tallahassee, and those ballots were run through the machines between eight and ten times. Now you take a punch card that has been punched through and run it through a machine that is designed to count it eight to ten times, you're going to get a lot of weird things happening to it. You go into those counting rooms and I've seen the photographs of them on the morning before they shipped the ballots to Tallahassee, and they are filled with chad all over the floor.

Some of them weren't votes in the presidential contest, but these ballots, particularly the punch cards, were not designed to be kept as accurate, immovable, immutable historical documents.

JAMIESON. But there's no reason to think that the machines would be Gore-biased and hence punching out the Gore chad. Wouldn't the machines be just throwing error across the process?

ROVE. That's right. That's my point. There is error across the process. In the early part of the process, go back and look at the film when Miami-Dade is thinking about doing the count. There's one judge bending the card, poking the card, striking the card. This is not a process designed to be impartial. Take a look at the votes. I'd be happy to supply any of you doing research on this with a complete list of the votes. The pattern of votes in these three counties, when they meet and when they talk about disputed ballots, is two to one Gore.

JAMIESON. There was a press account that said you had a strategy in the event that you had won the popular vote, but not the electoral vote, and that strategy had a communication component that potentially had advertising in it? Is that true?

ROVE. No. It was never discussed. It may have been discussed at a higher level of the campaign, like the interns and the mailroom clerks, but I never heard it discussed until I read it in the newspaper.

MARGARET KENSKI (Arizona Opinion). The Democrat institutional focus on the labor unions and minorities has been mentioned. Do you think that your dot-com approach is an effective counter to that, or do Republicans have to look to some other institutional base to counter what I assume the Democrats will continue to develop as a strategy in campaigns?

ROVE. One of my laundry list of mistakes in the campaign is the sense we had that we were going to beat them on turnout. Thank God, we had the largest, most extraordinary "get out the vote" effort we ever mounted. Otherwise we would have been swamped. We thought we would gain an advantage over them very early on by making a commitment to strengthen state party voter ID and "get out the vote" efforts, and take control of those party efforts with people in whom we had confidence in all the battleground states. We had twenty-eight battleground states. Only two of them were won by Bob Dole last time around. We did not worry about Oklahoma, Utah, Idaho, and Wyoming. Instead we looked at states that had been won by Clinton either once or twice. We didn't even worry about Montana. We looked at states like Nevada and Arizona and states that we thought would be in play, like Oregon, Washington, Iowa, Minnesota, and Wisconsin.

We started an extraordinary effort to raise money—particularly hard money, because a lot of these activities have to be undertaken with hard money—to do volunteer-intensive, "get out the vote" effort. We had a total budget of $57 million for the state parties. We had 939 headquarters staffed by 281 paid staff and 243,000 volunteers, whose names are all on computer. We had 207 people called "Bush Marshals." These were accomplished political people whom we recruited to take off a month or two in the fall to assign to an area to fill a need. There were communications people, political organizers, whatever. They were backed up by the "Mighty Victory Strike Force," as they named themselves. This was 1,725 people who took off a lesser amount of time to man headquarters or run a "get out the vote" operation or do door-to-door.

Our goal was to place 70 million phone calls in the last week of the campaign and we beat that by about 15 million. Our mail volume in the final week of the campaign was 111,544,186 pieces of mail. There were 60 different pieces of mail and they all hit. We had 16,500,000 pieces of literature dropped door-to-door in the last two weeks. 1,234,500 yard signs, 1,501,500 bumper stickers. I can tell you how many we had by state, if you like. Now, this effort was extraordinarily important to us. For example, we had 25 headquarters in West Virginia. This was extraordinarily important to us, allowing us to come close in a variety of states. A shift of 17,000 votes in New Mexico, Oregon, Iowa, and Wisconsin would have given us 30 more Electoral College votes. And what's interesting about those four states is that three of them were last won by the Republicans in 1984. In fact, we would have won New Mexico had it not been for snow. It snowed, unexpectedly, in the eastern part of New Mexico called "Little Texas," and they actually liked us there. Had it not snowed in that part of the state, we would have won.

Now, of course, on election night, some of the networks, in their infinite wisdom, called New Mexico for Gore. The next day it was found that a mere 55,000 votes had been overlooked in Bernalillo County and they had to recount. They had to add those in, and that changed it a little bit. But this grassroots effort was extraordinarily important to us. If Donna Brazile had not been with the Gore campaign, the full effect of this would have been clearly apparent to anybody. The fact that Donna, the AFL-CIO, NARAL, NOW, Handgun Control, and everybody else made an extraordinary effort allowed the success of our effort to be hidden a little.

FRANKOVIC. The New Mexico call was made very late at night. It was made based on what appeared to be almost complete total vote counts. This is not us jumping the gun. This is

Bernalillo County basically losing votes.

ROVE. The problem is Bernalillo County has done this for the last ten years. This is one of the most ill-run major county vote counting operations in the country, and not to look deeper is a problem.

FRANKOVIC. They found the extra votes the next day.

ROVE. Right. It took them eighteen hours from the time the polls closed to find the 55,000 votes.

FRANKOVIC. We called it because it looked like it was complete. We would have followed everybody's rules, wait until all the votes are in, when we called it and they still didn't get it right.

ROVE. Right. We may have won New Mexico, because it turned out that the counties that are predominantly Republican, that Bush did well in use optical scanners and there was a computer program that said if you voted straight ticket and voted for the presidential candidate, it kicked out your ballot. So we corrected this in one county, Chaves, Roswell, birthplace of Al Gore—at least that was what I read on the Internet.

The Internet was an interesting thing. Nowhere have I seen more funny jokes, weird gossip, and out-and-out falsehoods about both candidates circulate more quickly, more rapidly, and never be rebuttable, except on the Internet.

MONTAGUE KERN (Rutgers University). I've been very impressed with your data relating to turnout and these other sorts of things. I'm wondering about your data relating to the press. You started by talking about how you support Thomas Patterson's point of view. Do you base this on data that you've developed?

Do you have a way of looking at it? If so, what type of data? Second, other data suggest that the press was very favorable. A few reported during the earlier periods, very favorable, as we heard this morning, to Gore. Then after September 14, there was a strong tendency on the part of the press to focus on a different campaign perspective.

ROVE. I'm not the expert in this. An unnamed academic [Dr. Daron Shaw], now tenured at the University of Texas at Austin, who was hired by the Bush campaign, did content analysis. We had six students doing content analysis. What I derived from that is that there are ebbs and flows in the coverage that each candidate enjoyed. I also derived that what was being said when they came and went to local areas was almost more important than what the national network said. There are places like Florida, for example, where I didn't care what we did. We got negative coverage when we went to Florida from the print press.

KERN. But this was not uniform negative coverage.

ROVE. No, but the general nature of the tone of the coverage was very much in keeping with what Patterson suggests, that it is process oriented, highly cynical, negative, dismissive of issue positions, focused on the internals of the campaign and not on the big messages and really serves to trivialize the whole contest. They did a better job. I will grant you that, but they didn't do as good a job as they should, except for Rick Berke at the *New York Times*.

MICHAEL HAGEN (University of Pennsylvania). I have the impression that this was perhaps the most tightly targeted presidential campaign in history. Is that true? If it is, what makes that possible?

ROVE. Well, I don't know if it's true or not, but it was very highly targeted and what makes it possible is two words. Matthew Dowd.

We had our own in-house. Between him and Daron Shaw, we had every election by county, going back to 1970. We were able to do a lot of media market analysis and key state analysis. It identified pockets of swing voters for us, and allowed us to narrowly target phones and mail as well as television. It also allowed us to target candidate visits. In fact, ironically enough, the Gore campaign beat us on one important bit of targeting, which was that the more important part of Iowa is eastern Iowa. They took the river cruise, and unfortunately we could not target most of eastern Iowa, because none of the important runways in Dubuque and other cities would take a 757. They were smart. We sat there and said, "Oh, that boat, that's going to be a waste of time." But we started looking at the runways and said, "There is no way we're going to be able to get into Dubuque or Waterloo."

In Iowa, which we last won in 1984, we came within less than three-tenths of one percent of winning the state. The reason is we overperformed in the west, we overperformed in Polk County, Des Moines, but as you get to the east, we began to perform at level or below level, because we couldn't take the candidate there.

HAGEN. Could you revise your targets more quickly this time around than you have been able to in the past? What kind of technology made that possible?

ROVE. I'm not the expert. I simply looked at the product and said, "God, these guys are smart."

MATTHEW DOWD (Bush campaign). It's not rocket science.

It's a lot of thought, but you could do it with an Excel program and some other minor computer stuff.

ROVE. We had SPSS, too, and a couple other things. Did I sound like the I knew what the hell I was talking about there?

It allowed us to carefully target the visits of the candidate. I love the media. The final day of the campaign they say, "Oh, God, you guys are just coasting. You're going to Chattanooga, Green Bay, Quad Cities, and Northwest Arkansas. You're just putting the finger in Gore's eye and a finger in Clinton's eye and noodling around the Midwest."

We were looking at the tracking data and the media markets and the impact of the advertising and saying, "Where can we eke out one more vote?"

Another one of our eight mistakes was that in the final week we missed out on the opportunity of maximizing the schedule more. Ten days before the election, we let Bush take the day off. We should not have. In the final four or five days, we should have added one additional stop a day, just to impact one additional media market. In Iowa, for example, if we had been able to go, not only to Quad Cities, but to Omaha or Des Moines one more time, we would have won the state. If we had been able to go La Crosse or Eau Claire or Rhinelander or Madison one more time, we would have won Wisconsin. If we had been able to go to Roswell or Hobbs or Santa Fe or Farmington . . . actually, we did go to Farmington. We sent President Bush from Palm Springs in a little airplane to Farmington, New Mexico, and won Farmington by a huge number because it was the only time anybody showed up to campaign there. But if we had one more visit in New Mexico, we would have found those 366 votes.

But being able to carefully target and to know where we ought to go was very important. We were limited only by whether or not the runway would take a 757, or in the case of Cheney, a 727.

ERIKA PROSPER (Garcia LKS). What were the other six mistakes?

ROVE. Let me just run through them.

The early debate put us off stride. We thought the media would hold Gore to his very explicit promises to go on *Meet the Press*.

Conventions. We held ours first, they held theirs second. I wish it had been the other way around.

I alluded to GOTV earlier. Donna Brazile did a fabulous job. We did a fabulous job, but we should have done more. Plus we thought we were going to outmaneuver her on turnout, but we underestimated how much maneuvering she was going to do.

The mix of TV messages. This is one I can argue round and argue flat. Gore ended with a much more negative burst of messages. My sense is that the importance of television was not the message itself, but whether you were canceling out the other guy's message. We won in Florida because we were on in Miami and Jacksonville and Panama City and Pensacola more than Gore was, and in some cases exclusively. They were coming at us with exceptionally negative messages, particularly about four days before the election. In retrospect, should we have been doing more in that period of time?

Despite our targeting tools, the tactical focus was sometimes lost. I should have shored up the ground game in Florida earlier and put us into Florida earlier. Lieberman was not the key. It was Gore. Lieberman may have energized the "Condo Commandos" in Palm Beach and Broward and Miami Dade—that's their title, not mine—but you need to keep Lieberman in perspective. We increased the percentage of the Jewish vote won by the Republican presidential ticket from 16 to 19. You would have thought, with the hubbub about Lieberman, it would have continued to decline, but it didn't. But tactically, we missed a few bets like that.

Oregon, for example. In Oregon, they vote by mail and by ballot. People would show up at rallies with their ballots, and the practice is to send people through the crowd to collect them. We had reports at our first rally that there were people collecting ballots, but there was a question whether they were really our people. We sloughed it off, but they weren't our people. A whole series of little tactical miscues like that that cost us the state.

Finally, in the primaries, I'm convinced we could have done better. We might not have won New Hampshire, but we could have done better. We might have won New Hampshire had we been able to show up for the first debate, but that was impossible. It was scheduled on the day Laura Bush was being honored by SMU, her alma mater, and there was no way George W. Bush would leave his wife's side to go to a political event. But had we been able to attend the first debate, and spent more time in New Hampshire, we would have done better. That would have created a different dynamic for the primary and for the general election.

But there were lots of things we did well. The fact that we won is a sign that we did a lot of things well. We should have lost this election. It was a time of enormous peace and prosperity, and gaining 11.3 million votes happened only four times in the twentieth century: in 1948, after a four-way split; in 1972, after a three-way split; in 1976, after the Democrats were wiped out in the '72 campaign; and in 1984, after the three-way battle of 1980 with Reagan winning a huge vote. For Bush to climb back in the face of peace and prosperity with this huge shift of votes—11.3 million additional votes—is a pretty strong testament to the candidate and his message.

Participants

The contributors to this volume were discussants in the conference on campaign decision-making held at the Annenberg School for Communication, University of Pennsylvania, on February 10, 2001. A full list of the participants at this debriefing appears below.

Richard Berke, *New York Times*
David Birdsell, Baruch College
Henry Brady, University of California
Bruce Buchanan, University of Texas
Edward Carmines, University of Indiana
Karlyn Kohrs Campbell, University of Minnesota
Michael Delli Carpini, Pew Charitable Trusts
Alex Castellanos, Bush campaign
Matthew Dowd, Bush campaign
David Eisenhower, University of Pennsylvania
Carter Eskew, Gore campaign
Kathleen Frankovic, CBS News
Curtis Gans, Committee for the Study of the American Electorate
Joyce Garczynski, Annenberg School
Alan Gerber, Yale University
Dana Goldthwaite, Annenberg School
Doris Graber, University of Illinois, Chicago
Stanley Greenberg, Gore campaign
Michael Hagen, University of Pennsylvania
Kathleen Hall Jamieson, University of Pennsylvania
Richard Johnston, University of British Columbia
Elihu Katz, University of Pennsylvania
Henry Kenski, University of Arizona
Kate Kenski, Annenberg School

Margaret Kenski, Arizona Opinion
Montague Kern, Rutgers University
Kimberly Kirn, Annenberg School
Bill Knapp, Gore campaign
Ruth Mandel, Rutgers University
Thomas Mann, Brookings Institution
Carolyn Marvin, University of Pennsylvania
Mark McKinnon, Bush campaign
Tali Mendelberg, Princeton University
Brett Mueller, Annenberg School
Jack Nagel, University of Pennsylvania
Dan Orr, Annenberg School
Erika Prosper, Garcia LKS
Karl Rove, Bush campaign
Martin Seligman, University of Pennsylvania
Daron Shaw, University of Texas
Bob Shrum, Gore campaign
Herb Simons, Temple University
Alexander Slater, Annenberg School
Kathy Sosa, Garcia LKS
Lionel Sosa, Bush campaign
Fred Steeper, Bush campaign
Laura Stoker, University of California
Svjetlana Tepavcevic, Annenberg School
Paul Waldman, University of Pennsylvania
Claire Wardle, Annenberg School
Theodore Windt, University of Pittsburgh
Stanton Wortham, University of Pennsylvania

Index